Tax and Estate Planning Series

PLANNING
AN ESTATE
Second Edition

A GUIDEBOOK OF PRINCIPLES AND TECHNIQUES

**Cumulative supplement for use during 1987
Current to May 31, 1987**

Harold Weinstock
Member of the California Bar

> *Insert in the pocket at the
> back of the bound volume.
> Discard supplement dated 1986.*

D1457719

 Shepard's/McGraw-Hill, Inc.
P.O. Box 1235
Colorado Springs, Colorado 80901

Supplement ISBN 0-07-069051-0

Introduction
To 1987 Supplement

Since the completion of the manuscript for the text, there have been important developments in the estate planning field. In addition to judicial decisions and Internal Revenue Service rulings, Congress enacted the Tax Equity and Fiscal Responsibility Act of 1982, the Technical Corrections Act of 1982, the Subchapter S Revision Act of 1982, the Deficit Reduction Act of 1984 (which includes the Tax Reform Act of 1984) and the Tax Reform Act of 1986. These developments have an important effect on portions of the text.

The manuscript for this supplement was completed on May 31, 1987, and is, therefore, current as of that date. I would like to thank my legal assistant, Roslyn Perlmutter, for her help in reviewing the manuscript and making valuable suggestions, and my secretary, Sharon M. Sanderson, for typing the original and revisions of the manuscript.

Harold Weinstock
Los Angeles, California
May, 1987

iii

New sections in this supplement

Introduction to
Estate Planning

1

III. Occupations Involved in Estate Planning

§1.5   A. The Estate Planning Team

The last sentence (including the citation) of the last paragraph on page 4 is deleted and the following inserted:

It is estimated that 250 of these councils, with almost 23,000 members, belong to the National Association of Estate Planning Councils.

VII.   Recommended Reading

Insert after Eierman and McGarry in the recommended reading list on page 15:

Frazer, "Five Myths of Estate Planning" 124 No 12 *Trusts and Estates* 16 (1985).

Overview of Tax Principles

2

III. The Federal Estate Tax

§2.3 A. Steps to Follow in Making Computation

At the end of the second full paragraph on page 19, add:

The Internal Revenue Service takes the position that a decedent's gifts can be revalued for the purpose of the addback to the estate tax basis, even though a gift tax was paid on those gifts and the gift tax statute of limitations has expired. Letter Rul. 8447005.

B. Property Includable in Gross Estate

§2.5 1. Property Owned at Time of Death

At the end of the text, add:

Federal public housing agency bonds owned by a decedent who died prior to June 19, 1984 are, however, excludable from the gross estate. See *Haffner v US* 85-1 USTC ¶13,611 (7th Cir 1985); §641 of the Tax Reform Act of 1984.

2.   Property Transferred by Decedent During His Lifetime

§2.12   a. Gifts Made within Three Years of Death

At the end of the first paragraph on page 22, add the following sentence:

The Technical Corrections Act of 1982 amended I.R.C. §2035(d)(2) to provide that the transfers discussed in §§2.13, 2.14 and 2.15 (but not in §2.8) are includable in the gross estate regardless of whether or not they exceed the $10,000 annual gift tax exclusion.

§2.16   3. Valuation of Includable Assets

The first two sentences of the first paragraph on page 24 are changed to read:

Generally, the value of property included in the gross estate will be the fair market value at the date of death, that is, the price at which a willing seller will sell and a willing buyer who has knowledge of the facts will purchase, neither being under any compulsion to buy or sell. Under I.R.C. §2032, if both the value of the gross estate and the estate tax are reduced as a result, the estate representative may elect to value the property included in the gross estate as of six months after the date of death.

At the end of the text on page 24, add:

I.R.C. §6660, enacted in 1984, imposes a penalty for understatement of the estate and gift taxes resulting from undervaluation of property. The penalty is a percentage of the underpayment of tax computed as follows:

Ratio of Claimed Valuation to Correct Valuation	Penalty Percentage
50% or more but not more than 66-2/3%	10%
40% or more but less than 50%	20%
Less than 40%	30%

C.   Deductions from Gross Estate

§2.22   3. Marital Deduction

The second sentence of the second paragraph on page 25 is changed to read:

A qualifying terminable interest requires that the surviving spouse be entitled to receive all the income from the property at least annually and that no person be able to appoint the property during the spouse's lifetime to anyone other than the spouse.

§2.24A   6. Deduction for Proceeds from the Sale of Employer Securities (New)

The Tax Reform Act of 1986 permits the deduction from the gross estate of an amount equal to 50 per cent of the proceeds of the sale of employer securities to ESOPs (see §13.13) made prior to the due date of the estate tax return (including extension of time). I.R.C. §2057. This provision, as enacted, is due to expire on January 1, 1992. For the deduction to be allowed, the sale must be made by the executor and the securities cannot have been acquired by the decedent from an ESOP or through other specified employee transactions. The Internal Revenue Service has stated that it will deny the deduction if the securities were purchased by the estate after the decedent's death or if the securities, after purchase by the ESOP, are not distributed to the employee participants in the plan. Notice 87-13, I.R.B. 1987-4 (Jan 26, 1987). While the Internal Revenue Service's position appears to go beyond the statutory language, the estate planner should be aware of the likelihood that the Internal Revenue Code may be amended to restrict the deduction.

V.   The Federal Gift Tax

§2.37   C. Transfer Subject to the Gift Tax

At the end of the text on page 32, add:

For the tax penalty which is imposed for undervaluation of the value of the gift, see Supplement §2.16.

§2.47 VI. State Gift Taxes

The first sentence on page 35 is changed to read:

Eight states currently impose a gift tax.[1]

Footnote 1, on page 35, is changed to read:

[1] Delaware, Louisiana, New York, North Carolina, Oregon, Rhode Island, South Carolina, Tennessee, Vermont, and Wisconsin.

VII. Basis of Property for Federal Income Tax Purposes

§2.48 A. Property Acquired from a Decedent

At the end of the text on page 36, add:

Assets subject to the generation-skipping transfer tax (see Supplement §§5.34 to 5.42) also generally receive a new basis equal to the fair market value of the assets at the time the generation-skipping transfer tax is imposed. See I.R.C. §2654(a).

§2.51 B. Property Acquired by Gift

At the end of the second paragraph on page 37, add:

I.R.C. §2654(a) also allows an increase in basis for the generation-skipping transfer tax paid on the transfer, but the increase is limited to the portion of the tax by which the fair market value exceeds the donor's adjusted basis immediately before the gift.

The following paragraph is added at the end of the text:

When one spouse sells to or exchanges an asset with the other spouse, the transaction is not treated like a sale or exchange, but as if the transferee received the property by gift. Accordingly, the transferee takes the transferor's basis in the property. I.R.C. §1041(b).

§2.52   C. Holding Period

The following sentence is inserted between the first and second sentences of the first paragraph on page 37:

However, if the asset was purchased after June 22, 1984, but before January 1, 1988, the holding period for long-term capital gain or loss is more than six months, rather than more than one year.

At the end of the text on page 38, add:

The Tax Reform Act of 1986 repealed the exclusion of 60 per cent of net long-term capital gains. Act §301. Accordingly, all net capital gains are includable in income, but may not be taxed at a rate in excess of 28 per cent. However, for years after 1987, the inclusion of capital gains in income may cause certain of the taxpayer's income to be taxed at the 33 per cent bracket resulting from the phase-out of the benefit of the 15 per cent tax rate or the personal exemption. See I.R.C. §1(g) and (j). Capital losses, whether long-term or short-term, can offset up to $3,000 of ordinary income. Act §301(b).

Planning a Small Family Estate

3

III. Planning for the Minor Children on the Death of the Surviving Spouse

B. Providing Management and Conservation of the Children's Property

1. Appointment of a Guardian of the Estate

§3.16   a. Disadvantages of the Guardianship of the Estate

Item 1 on page 45 is changed to read:

1. A guardianship bond may be required and its cost must be borne by the guardianship estate.

Item 7 on page 45 is added:

7.   If the minor dies prior to the termination of the guardianship, the guardianship assets will be payable to the minor's probate estate. As a result, the assets will pass to the minor's beneficiaries rather than to the estate owner's beneficiaries, who may not, in all cases, be the same persons.

§3.20   2. Transfers under Custodian Statute (New)

An alternative to the use of a trust to avoid a guardianship of the estate of a minor is for the estate owner, where permitted by state law, to make a testamentary transfer (either by will or trust) to a custodian for the minor. Various states have adopted the Uniform Transfers to Minors Act, which is similar to the Uniform Gifts to Minors Act (see §§8.27 to 8.31), but permits testamentary transfers as well as lifetime gifts. (For example, see Cal. Prob. Code §3905). The estate owner in his or her will or trust may designate the custodian or leave the decision of selecting the custodian to the executor or trustee.

The custodian will administer the estate of the minor without the necessity of court intervention, thereby avoiding court costs, delays, and the necessity of the court accounting. However, the disadvantages of a guardianship, listed in items 4 through 7 in §3.16 and supplement §3.16, are also generally present in custodianship administration. Some states permit the estate owner to specify that the custodianship will terminate when the minor reaches age 21 (or even 25, see Cal. Prob. Code §3920.5), rather than age 18.

Obtaining the Marital Deduction and the Community Property Exclusion to Save Death Taxes

4

II. Marital Deduction

B. Computing the Maximum Marital Deduction

§4.4   2. Computation Under Pre-September 12, 1981 Formula Maximum Marital Deduction Clause

The heading on page 51 is changed to read:

2. Computation Under Pre-September 13, 1981 Formula Maximum Marital Deduction Clause

The first sentence on page 51 is changed to read:

The unlimited marital deduction will not apply automatically to a decedent's will or trust dated before September 13, 1981, if it contains a formula clause expressly providing for a marital deduction bequest to the spouse.

The last sentence on page 52 is changed to read:

For a description of how to compute the maximum marital deduction in those estates where the estate owner, deliberately or otherwise, failed to amend his or her pre-September 13, 1981 will or trust which contains a formula marital deduction clause, see §§4.5 to 4.7.

§4.8   C. To What Extent Should the Marital Deduction Be Used?

The first full sentence on page 56 should be changed to read:

To illustrate, if the husband divided his estate so that $675,000 went to the "A" trust and $675,000 to the "B" trust, there would be a tax of $27,750 on his death and a tax of $27,750 on the wife's subsequent death, or a total of $55,500 on both deaths, which is no less than the amount which would have been paid if there had been a total deferral of the tax on the first death.

E.   How To Qualify for the Marital Deduction

1.   Avoid the Terminable Interest Rule

c.   "Power of Appointment Trust"

§4.15   i. "Specific Portion"

Delete the second and third sentences of the second paragraph, on page 61, and insert the following:

The Tax Court held that a specific portion for this purpose is not limited to a fractional or percentile share. *Estate of CS Alexander v Commr* 82 TC 34 (1984) (affd by 4th Cir 1985, unpublished opinion under 4th Cir rules). For example, the surviving spouse may be given the right to appoint $100,000 of the principal upon his or her death. Unless the *Alexander* case is reversed on appeal, it will give rise to a valuable device. The decedent's will could give the surviving spouse the right to appoint that amount of principal which is equal to the marital deduction taken in the estate. When the surviving spouse dies, only such amount will be includable in that estate and any appreciation in the value of the principal during the surviving spouse's lifetime will pass free of estate tax on death.

   If the income interest and the general power are not in the same proportion, the marital deduction is limited to the smaller share. Reg. §20.2056(b)-5(b). For example, if the surviving spouse is entitled to only one-half the income, but has a power of appointment as to all the property, the marital deduction is limited to one-half the property.

§4.19 e. "Estate" Trust

The fifth and sixth paragraphs, on pages 63 and 64, are changed to read:

Another advantage of an estate trust is its greater flexibility if it distributes income in the form of appreciated assets. Unless the distribution is made to satisfy a specific sum required to be paid to the distributee under the trust instrument, the trustee, if he or she wishes, may avoid having the appreciation taxable to the trust as a gain. I.R.C. §643(d); Reg. §1.661(a)-2(f)(3); Rev. Rul. 67-74, 1967-1 C.B. 194. In the case of an estate trust, a distribution in kind will not be considered to be in satisfaction of a specific sum required to be distributed by the trust because of the trustee's power to accumulate current income. By way of example, assume that an estate trust has $10,000 of current income, and, instead of distributing this sum in cash, distributes an asset worth $10,000 with an income tax basis of $2,000. The beneficiary will include $2,000 in gross income, but will not, however, receive a new basis for the asset, and the trust will not realize any gain on the distribution. Alternatively, the trustee may elect to realize gain on the distribution. I.R.C. §643(d). In that case, the trust would realize a gain of $8,000, and the beneficiary would include $10,000 in gross income and receive a new basis of $10,000 for the asset.

However, where a power of appointment trust or "QTIP" trust (see §4.20) is used, the income must be distributed currently (see §4.16). Here, a distribution of appreciated assets may be deemed to be in satisfaction of a specific sum required to be distributed and thereby give rise to gain, taxable to the trust. In this situation, the trustee is not permitted to elect to avoid gain. Accordingly, using the same example given above in the case of a power of appointment trust, the trust will realize a taxable gain of $8,000, and the beneficiary will report income of $10,000 and receive a new basis of $10,000 for the asset.

f. "QTIP" Trust

§4.22 ii. Executor's Election

The last sentence on page 65 is deleted and the following is inserted:

Under proposed regulations, the executor may, if he or she wishes, elect to deduct only a portion of the bequest left to a "QTIP" trust. Proposed Reg §20.2056(b)-7(b). However, such partial election must relate to a fractional or percentile share of the property as opposed to a fixed dollar amount. The fractional or percentile share may be defined by means of a formula. As a result, the executor should, for example, be able to limit the election to only that portion of the "QTIP" trust assets which will eliminate the federal estate tax after applying the other deductions and credits to which the estate is entitled. Letter Rul. 8301050.

§4.24   iv. Other Planning Considerations

At the end of the third paragraph on page 66 add:

The Technical Corrections Act of 1982 amended the code to provide that the "QTIP" assets receive a new basis on the surviving spouse's death. I.R.C. §1014(b)(10). As a result, appreciated assets will receive a step up in basis.

An additional consideration is whether the decedent's residence may be placed in the "QTIP" trust. The lifetime right to use and occupy a residence will qualify as an income interest. Proposed Reg §20.2056(b)-7(e). However, if the home is sold after the surviving spouse reaches age 55, the gain exclusion of up to $125,000 (see I.R.C. §121) may not be available to the spouse. Cf. Rev. Rul. 84-43, 1984-1 C.B. 27.

F.   Formula Clause Marital Deduction Bequest

§4.26   1. Description

At the end of the third paragraph, on page 67, add the following paragraph:

It is also important to note that if the marital deduction bequest is to a "QTIP" trust (see §4.20), special care must be taken in drafting the formula clause. The clause should clearly state that the bequest is to pass to the "QTIP" trust even though the "QTIP" election is not actually made by the executor. See §4.22. If this language is not inserted, the Internal Revenue Service may disallow the marital deduction where the assets, upon the failure of the executor to make the "QTIP" election, would pass to other beneficiaries. See Letter Rul. 8611006.

4. Selecting the Appropriate Formula Clause

§4.30 a. Strict Pecuniary Clause

The following is added at the end of the sixth line from the top of page 70:

But see §7.32, for a discussion of the disallowance of the loss when the distribution comes from a funded revocable living trust rather than from a probate estate.

§4.31 b. Fractional Share of the Residue Clause

Item 2 on page 72 is changed to read:

2. In the typical fractional share of the residue clause, there is no opportunity to allocate growth assets to the residuary trust and relatively fixed value assets to the marital trust, as there is under a pecuniary type bequest. (See §§4.30 and 4.32.) In order to achieve flexibility, such a clause may, however, be modified to give discretionary authority to the fiduciary to allocate assets in kind based on the date of distribution values, rather than to allocate an undivided interest in each and every asset. When the authority is vested in the fiduciary, and not in the beneficiaries, no gain will be realized to the estate or the beneficiaries upon such a non-pro rata distribution. See Rev. Rul. 55-117, 1955-1 C.B. 233; Letter Ruls. 7929054, 8029054, and 8119040. If such a clause is used, a second valuation of the estate's assets must be made on the date of distribution.

   For example, if the estate, based on estate tax values, is $2,000,000, the marital deduction is $1,400,000 and the estate is worth $2,500,000 on the date of distribution, assets selected by the fiduciary worth 14/20ths of $2,500,000 or $1,750,000 may be allocated to the marital trust and assets worth 6/20ths of $2,500,000 or $750,000 may be allocated to the exemption bypass trust.

III.   Community Property Exclusion

§4.34   A. The Community Property System

The first sentence on page 74 is changed to read:

The community property system is in effect in nine states: namely, Arizona, California, Idaho, Louisiana, Nevada, New Mexico, Texas, Washington, and Wisconsin.

§4.36   C. Tax Exclusion of One-Half of the Community Property

The following sentence is inserted between the second and third sentences of the text on page 75:

The decedent's one-half may be entitled to a minority interest discount if it can be shown that a prospective purchaser would pay proportionately less for a one-half interest in the asset than he would pay for both halves. See *Estate of Propstra v US* 680 F2d 1248 (9th Cir. 1982).

IV.   Recommended Reading

Insert after Friedman in the recommended reading list on page 76:

Garlock, "Estate Tax Unlimited Marital Deduction Has Limited Advantages in Larger Estates" 4 *Journal of Taxation* 236 (1982).

Gorman, Hoffman & Weinstock, "The Marital Deduction: Beyond the Basics" 35 *Univ So Cal Tax Inst* 16-1 (1983).

Bypassing the Second Tax

5

II.   Maximum Benefit Trust

B.   Rights and Benefits to Wife in "B" Trust

§5.4   1. Power to Invade Under an Ascertainable Standard

At the end of the second to the last sentence of the first paragraph on page 82 add:

This case was reversed on appeal. 708 F2d 1564 (10th Cir 1983).

§5.6   3. Special Power to Appoint to Third Parties

The last paragraph on page 85 is deleted and the following paragraph is inserted in place thereof:

The special power to appoint to third persons will cause adverse tax consequences where the wife, by disclaimer, permits a certain portion of the marital deduction bequest to fall into the "B" trust. See §4.8. The disclaimer is not a qualified one under I.R.C. §2518, because it fails to satisfy the statutory requirement that the disclaimed assets pass without any direction on the part of the disclaiming party. I.R.C. §2518(b)(4). Also see §15.40. Because the disclaimer is not a qualified one, the disclaimed assets will be included in the wife's estate.

§5.8   D. Gift Tax

At the end of the carryover paragraph on page 86, add:

See also Reg. §25.2514-1(b)(2); *Estate of Regester* 83 TC 1 (1984).

III.   Discretionary Trust

B.   Specific Considerations

§5.13   2. Substantial Owner Under I.R.C. §678

The first sentence on page 87 is changed to read:

The wife, even when she is not a trustee, may suffer income tax consequences if she has the power, whether or not exercised, to invade the principal of the discretionary "B" trust despite the fact that her power is a noncumulative power to invade up to $5,000 or 5 per cent, whichever is greater.

§5.14   3. Trustee with a Sprinkling Power Should Not Also Be a Beneficiary

At the end of the runover paragraph on page 88 add:

The Internal Revenue Service may possibly take the position that the wife will be deemed to have exercised a general power of appointment when a third party trustee has broad discretionary powers, even if the wife's power to substitute trustees is limited to appointing a third person or even a corporate trustee. See Rev. Rul. 79-353, 1979-2 C.B. 325; but see *First National Bank of Denver v US* 648 F2d 1286 (10th Cir 1981).

IV. Widow's (or Widower's) Election Trust

C. Tax Consequences of "Traditional" Widow's Election

§5.19 1. Death Taxes on the Husband's Death

At the end of the text on page 91 add:

Because of new valuation tables (see Appendix VIII of the Supplement for an explanation), new calculations should be substituted in the example in the text . Under the facts of the example, at age 65, the value of the widow's remainder interest would be $320,300 ($1,000,000 times .32030, see Supplement Appendix VIII, Table A), instead of $441,970, and the allowable amount of the marital deduction would be $629,700 rather than $508,030. If the wife were age 80, the value of the widow's remainder interest would be $563,410, instead of $698,830.

If, because of the size of the estate or the age of the wife, a meaningful reduction in the amount of the marital deduction will take place, an alternative can be considered to prevent such reduction. If the bypass trust provides for income for life to the wife, such income interest, rather than the marital bequest, may serve as the consideration for the wife exchanging at least a portion of her remainder interest. To the extent that the marital deduction bequest is not dependent upon the wife giving up anything, the full marital deduction will be allowed on the husband's death.

§5.20 2. Gift Tax to Widow

The second sentence of the third paragraph on page 91 is changed to read:

There will have been an undue reduction in the amount of the marital deduction and, at the same time, because the retention of the power of appointment will cause her one-half of the community property to be included in her gross estate, the optimum estate tax benefit on her subsequent death will not have been achieved. See §§5.16 and 5.24.

At the end of the text on page 91 add:

Because of new valuation tables (see Appendix VIII of the Supplement for an explanation), new calculations should be substituted in the example in the text. Under the facts of the example, the remainder interest surrendered is worth $320,300 ($1,000,000 times .32030) and the income interest received is worth $645,715 ($950,000 times .67907)(see Supplement Appendix VIII, Table A). If the widow were age 80, there would be a taxable gift to the remaindermen of $148,649.

3.   Income Taxes

§5.22   a. Income Tax to the Widow

At the end of the text on page 93 add:

Because of new valuation tables (see Appendix VIII of the Supplement for an explanation), new calculations should be submitted in the example in the text. Accordingly, the third paragraph on page 92 is changed to read:

Using the facts of the basic example (see §§5.18 and 5.20), where the value of the widow's remainder interest on the date of the exchange is $320,300 and the value of the income interest in the husband's estate is $645,715, and assuming that the basis of the widow's remainder interest is $300,000, the taxable gain to the widow will be $20,300 ($320,300 minus $300,000). The amount by which the value of the income interest exceeds the value of the remainder interest—i.e., $325,415 ($645,715 minus $320,300)—constitutes a testamentary gift from the husband to the widow. Conversely, if the value of the income interest in the husband's estate were only $310,000, the taxable gain would be $10,000 ($310,000 minus $300,000). In the latter situation, the amount by which the value of the widow's remainder interest exceeds the value of the income interest in the husband's estate—i.e., $10,300 ($320,300 minus $310,000)—will be a taxable gift by the widow (see §5.20). Whatever the amount of the gain, it will be long-term capital gain even if the exchange takes place immediately after the husband's death. I.R.C. §§1223(11) and 1014(b)(6).

The last sentence of the carryover paragraph on page 93 is changed to read:

The amortization deduction, by reference to the facts in the basic example (see §5.18), is computed by dividing the value of the widow's remainder interest ($320,300, see §5.20) by the wife's life expectancy (18.2 years, see Table I, Reg. §1.72-9), or $17,599 per year.

§5.23 b. Income Tax Consequences to Husband's Estate

Because of new valuation tables (see Appendix VIII of the Supplement for an explanation), new calculations should be substituted in the example in the text. Accordingly, the reference to $441,970 in the fifth sentence of the first paragraph on page 93 should be changed to $320,300.

§5.24 4. Death Taxes at the Widow's Death

At the end of the second paragraph on page 94 add:

In an 1987 Court of Claims case, *Gradow v US* 87-1 USTC ¶13,711 (Ct Cl 1987), the court held that, because a widow's election is essentially a testamentary device to leave both one-halves of the community property to the children and yet avoid an estate tax on the survivor's one-half, the transfer is not for full consideration, unless the value of the consideration is at least equal to the total value of the wife's one-half of the community property and not merely the value of the remainder interest in such one-half. If this case remains good law, the estate tax benefit of the traditional widow's election will be largely negated. However, see Supplement §5.30; see also §8.48.

D. The "New" Widow's Election

2. Tax Consequences of the "New" Widow's Election

§5.28 b. Gift Taxes to Widow

At the end of the text on page 95 add:

Because of new valuation tables (see Appendix VIII of the Supplement for an explanation), new calculations should be substituted in the example in the text. Accordingly, if the widow were 108 years old, the value of her remainder interest would be $899,320. (See Supplement Appendix VIII, Table A.)

§5.30   d. Death Taxes on Widow's Death

At the end of the text on page 96, add:

In a 1987 Court of Claims case, *Gradow v US* 87-1 USTC ¶13,711 (Ct Cl 1987), the court held that, because a widow's election is essentially a testamentary device to leave both halves of the community property to the children and yet avoid an estate tax on the survivor's one-half, the transfer is not for full consideration, unless the value of the consideration is at least equal to the total value of the wife's one-half of the community property and not merely the value of the remainder interest in such one-half. In most instances, this holding will not have an adverse effect on the "new" widow's election because the consideration received by the wife will consist of the principal value of the husband's one-half of the community property and not merely an income interest therein. The husband's one-half will theoretically equal the full value of the wife's one-half of the community property. As a practical matter, however, the husband's one-half may fall somewhat short of half of the community property, because the husband's one-half will be charged with administration expenses resulting from his death. The widow's election can, however, be drafted as a measured widow's election to insure that whatever the consideration given by the husband, it will be full and adequate for what the widow gives up. The husband merely has to require the widow to exchange a portion of her remainder interest in her one-half of the community property rather than her entire remainder interest. The portion which she is required to exchange will be defined as that portion of the total value of her one-half of the community property which is no greater than the value of the net consideration received from the husband.

V.   Bypass Trust for Beneficiaries other than Spouses

B.   Generation-Skipping Transfer Tax

Sections 5.34 through 5.39 on pages 97 to 100 of the text are deleted and in place thereof the following sections are inserted:

§5.34   1. In General

The Tax Reform Act of 1986 retroactively repealed the generation-skipping transfer tax which had been in effect since 1976 and enacted a new and significantly different generation-skipping transfer tax in its place.

In general terms, the new generation-skipping transfer tax is imposed whenever there is a transfer to a person more than one generation below that of the transferor. The policy reason for imposition of this tax is to deter an estate owner from skipping the members of the immediately lower generation and thereby depriving the government of an estate tax on the death of a member of such immediately lower generation. For example, assume A makes a gift or leaves a bequest to his grandchildren. The gifted assets will be subject not only to gift tax (or, in the case of a bequest, to estate tax), but also to a generation-skipping transfer tax. By way of another example, assume A creates a trust for B, his child, with income to B for life, and on B's death the trust assets to go to B's children. Upon B's death the trust assets will not be included in B's estate, but will be subject to the generation-skipping transfer tax.

The generation-skipping transfer tax is imposed at a flat rate equal to the maximum estate tax rate, which is 55 per cent for persons dying during 1987 and 50 per cent for those dying thereafter. See Supplement §5.40 for a discussion of the exemptions and exclusions which may be available in computing the tax.

§5.35   2. What is a Generation-Skipping Transfer?

A *generation-skipping transfer*, giving rise to the generation-skipping transfer tax, is a transfer to or for the benefit of a *skip person*, which means a person who is more than one generation removed from the transferor. I.R.C. §2613.

Generally, a generation is determined along family lines. For example, the transferor, his wife, and his brothers and sisters are one generation; their children (including adopted children) are the first "younger generation," and the grandchildren constitute the second "younger generation." Husbands and wives of family members are assigned to the same generation as their spouses. I.R.C. §2651(b) and (c). However, a transfer to a grandchild whose deceased parent was the child of the transferor or the transferors' spouse is not considered to be a transfer to a skip person. I.R.C. §2612(c)(2). In that case the grandchild is deemed to belong to the child's generation.

Where generation-skipping transfers are made outside the family, generations are to be measured from the grantor. Individuals not more than 12-1/2 years younger than the grantor are treated as members of the grantor's generation. Individuals more than 12-1/2 years younger than the grantor, but not more than 37-1/2 years younger, are considered members of his children's generation. I.R.C. §2651(d).

§5.36   3. When and on What Base Is the Tax Imposed?

The time when and the amount on which the generation-skipping transfer tax is imposed depends upon whether the generation-skipping transfer is a direct skip, a taxable distribution, or a taxable termination. See Supplement §§5.37 to 5.39.

§5.37   a. Direct Skip

A *direct skip* is a transfer to a skip person subject to gift tax or estate tax (see Supplement §5.35). I.R.C. §2612(c).

The most common example of a direct skip is an outright gift to a grandchild. If the gift is made in trust all the current beneficiaries (except for holders of nominal interests) must be skip persons, otherwise the transfer is not deemed to be a direct skip. Accordingly, if the trust provides that income may be distributed to a grandchild *and* to a child of the transferor, the transfer is not a direct skip. However, if the trust provides that the grandchild receives the income and the remainder on the grandchild's death goes to the transferor's child, the skip person is the only current beneficiary and the transfer is a direct skip.

If the transfer is a direct skip, the generation-skipping transfer tax is imposed at the time of the transfer. If it is a lifetime gift, the tax is imposed when the gift is made; if it is a death transfer, at the time of the transferor's death. The tax is payable by the transferor or his estate.

The generation-skipping transfer tax imposed is in addition to the gift tax or the estate tax. In the case of a lifetime gift, the value of the gift for gift tax purposes is increased by the generation-skipping transfer tax. I.R.C. §2515. In each case, the generation-skipping transfer tax is based on the net amount received by the transferee. I.R.C. §2623. For example, A, from his $3,000,000 estate, after otherwise using up all exemptions and exclusions, leaves $100,000 to his grandchild. Assuming the estate tax top bracket is 50 per cent and his will directs that each beneficiary be charged with a pro-rata portion of the estate tax, the net amount which the grandchild will receive is $50,000. The generation-skipping transfer tax will be $25,000 (50 per cent times $50,000). However, one should realize that the tax on a direct skip is computed on a tax-exclusive basis. The estate, which is liable for the tax, will pay the $25,000 tax out of other assets. Thus, the tax is, in reality, 33-1/3 per cent of the total transfer of $75,000.

§5.38   b. Taxable Termination

A *taxable termination* is the termination of a beneficiary's interest in trust property as a result of death, lapse of time, or otherwise unless:

1. Immediately after the termination, a nonskip person has an interest in the property, or
2. No distribution may be made after the termination from the trust to a skip person. I.R.C. §2612(a)(1).

Under this definition, if A creates a trust which provides that the income is to go to A's child and upon the child's death, the principal to A's grandchildren, there would be a taxable termination upon the child's death.

When the generation-skipping transfer results from a taxable termination, the taxable amount is the value of the property with respect to which the termination has occurred, less applicable expenses and debts. I.R.C. §2622. The tax is imposed at the time of the termination and is payable by the trustee. I.R.C. §2603(a)(2). Hence, the tax is on an inclusive basis. If the taxable amount is $75,000, the tax, assuming a 50 per cent rate, will be $37,500 and the beneficiaries will receive $37,500. For an example of the computation of the tax on an exclusive basis, see Supplement §5.37.

§5.39 c. Taxable Distribution

A *taxable distribution* is any distribution from a trust to a skip person, which is not a direct skip or a taxable termination (see Supplement §§5.37 and 5.38). I.R.C. §2612(b). For example, assume the trust provides that the trustee is authorized to pay income and/or principal to the transferor's children and grandchildren. A distribution, before the final termination of the trust, is made to a grandchild, who is a skip person. This distribution is a taxable distribution.

The taxable amount in the case of a taxable distribution is the value of the property received by the transferee, less any expense incurred by the transferee in connection with the determination, collection, or refund of the generation-skipping transfer tax imposed by the distribution. I.R.C. §2621. The tax is imposed at the time of the distribution and is payable by the transferee. Thus, the tax is computed on a tax-inclusive basis (see Supplement §5.38). I.R.C. §2603(a)(1). If the tax is paid out of the trust, the amount of the tax is treated as an additional taxable distribution and there will be a generation-skipping transfer tax on that amount as well. I.R.C. §2621(b).

§5.40 4. Exemptions and Exclusions

The following exemptions and exclusions are allowable in computing the generation-skipping transfer tax:

1. Lifetime gifts which are excludable in computing the gift tax are also excludable in computing the generation-skipping transfer tax. These gifts include annual exclusion gifts (see §§2.38 and 2.39) and gifts for medical payments and tuition (see §2.41) I.R.C. §2642(c)(3).

2. Each person who is a transferor is entitled to a $1,000,000 exemption. I.R.C. §2631(a). In the case of married couples who make lifetime gifts and elect gift-splitting (see §2.38), each spouse will be deemed to have made one-half of the gift and each will be entitled to up to a $1,000,000 exemption. I.R.C. §2652(a)(2). In the case of a death transfer, each spouse is treated as the transferor of his or her own estate and, except in the case of a "QTIP" trust (see §4.20), no part of the exemption belonging to either of them may be allocated to the other. If one spouse gives or leaves a portion of his estate to a "QTIP" trust for the other spouse, the assets in the "QTIP" trust are normally deemed to belong to the donee spouse for transfer tax purposes. I.R.C. §2044. However, under I.R.C. §2652(a)(3) a special election may be made by the donor or, if it is a death transfer, by his executor to treat the exemption, to the extent of the value of the property passing to the "QTIP" trust, as belonging to the donor spouse. For further discussion see Supplement §5.42.

    If the transferor creates more than one generation-skipping transfer during his life or upon his death, the $1,000,000 exemption may be allocated among the various transfers at any time prior to the due date of the transferor's federal estate tax return. I.R.C. §§2631 and 2632.

    Unless the aggregate transfers do not exceed the $1,000,000 exemption, it is possible that one or more of the transfers will be partially taxable and partially exempt. If that is the case, the generation-skipping transfer tax is computed by applying the 50 per cent rate (or 55 per cent, prior to 1988) to the nonexempt portion. For example, assume A dies and leaves an estate of $2,000,000 in trust with income for a child for life and on the child's death the remainder to go to the child's children. Assume the death taxes and expenses of the estate are $625,000, leaving a net of $1,375,000. The entire $1,000,000 exemption is allocated to this trust. Accordingly, 72.73 per cent ($1,000,000 - $1,375,000) of the trust is exempt and 27.27 per cent is not exempt. Assume that the child dies after 1987 and the trust assets are then worth $1,800,000. The generation-skipping transfer tax would be $245,430 (27.27 per cent × $1,800,000 × 50 per cent). (See Supplement §5.42 for a discussion of dividing the trust into two parts.)

3. There is a special exclusion of aggregate transfers to each grandchild for direct skips made before January 1, 1990. The exclusion is limited to $2,000,000 per grandchild. Section 1433(b)(3) of the Tax Reform Act of 1986. It is necessary that the transfer be made solely to the grandchild. As a result, if the transfer is made to a trust where the grandchild receives only the income, but does not have a vested interest in the principal, the exclusion will not be allowed. Although it is not entirely clear, it would appear that if the grandchild is to receive the income from the trust and has a general power of appointment over the principal, or the principal is distributable to the grandchild's estate on his death, the exclusion should be allowed.

§5.41   5. Effective Dates

The generation-skipping transfer tax is generally applicable to all generation-skipping lifetime transfers made after September 25, 1985. However, the tax does not apply if the lifetime transfer is made from a trust that was irrevocable on that date, except to the extent that an addition was made to the trust after such date. The estate owner should, therefore, not make any transfers to irrevocable trusts which were in existence prior to September 26, 1985.

The tax is applicable to all generation-skipping transfers made by a decedent dying on or after October 22, 1986. However, there is an exception for transfers occurring under a will (but not a revocable trust) executed before October 22, 1986, if the decedent did not change the will and in fact died before December 31, 1986.

§5.42   6. Planning under the Generation-Skipping Transfer Tax

One of the best ways to avoid the generation-skipping transfer tax is to plan the transfers so as to take full advantage of the applicable exemptions and exclusions. See Supplement §5.40. For example, assume that a married couple has two children, each of whom has one child. The couple has a $4,000,000 estate. They desire to leave their entire estate in the form of a maximum benefit (see §§4.8 and 5.2) A-B trust for the benefit of the surviving spouse and, when both spouses die, outright to the children. The couple should consider taking the following planning steps:

1. To take full advantage of the $1,000,000 exemption to which each transferor is entitled, the couple should make sure that of the total $4,000,000 estate, each spouse owns at least $1,000,000. Otherwise, if the spouse owning a smaller portion of the estate dies first, the full $1,000,000 exemption of that

spouse will not be available. The poorer spouse's estate can be increased by interspousal lifetime gifts, such gifts being exempt from gift taxation. See §8.14.

2. At least $400,000 of the marital deduction portion of the A-B trust should consist of a "QTIP" trust (see §4.20), rather than an outright bequest (see §4.12), a power of appointment trust (see §4.14), or an estate trust (see §4.19). If not for the use of a "QTIP" trust, the couple's total transfers or exemptions would be limited to $1,600,000, because when the first spouse dies only the $600,000 left to the "B" (by-pass) trust will qualify for the exemption. By using a "QTIP" trust for at least $400,000 and having the executor elect to treat the decedent as the transferor of that $400,000 (see Supplement §5.40), the exemption of the first spouse to die will be $1,000,000 instead of $600,000.

3. When the surviving spouse dies, that portion of the estate which will qualify for the transferor exemption (i.e., $1,000,000 for each spouse, or a total of $2,000,000), should go into trust for the children rather than outright to them. The trust could be divided into separate trusts, one for each child. Each trust could be a maximum-benefit type trust, permitting each child to be the trustee of his or her own trust and provide that the child receive the income for life, a power to invade principal under an ascertainable standard (see §5.4), and a special (but not general) power to appoint to third persons (see §5.6), and, on the child's death, if the power of appointment is not exercised, then to the child's children. As a result, on the child's death, the assets in the trust will be subject to neither federal estate tax nor to the generation-skipping transfer tax.

4. If the couple is so inclined, they could consider gifting, or on death, leaving exempt portions of their estate by way of direct skips to their grandchildren. If the gifts are made or the estate owner's death occurs prior to 1990, and the grandchildren receive vested interests in the gifts, a $2,000,000 per grandchild exclusion will be available. See Supplement §5.40.

In planning for generation-skipping transfers which are not wholly exempt, the following factors should be kept in mind:

1. When a transfer to a generation-skipping trust exceeds, or is likely to exceed, the amount of the exemptions and exclusions, the trustee should be authorized or directed to divide the trust into an exempt part and a nonexempt part. After the division, distributions and investment decisions can be made so as to minimize the generation-skipping transfer taxes. For example, assume a single person leaves $2,000,000 in trust for her child with remainder to grandchildren. If the full $1,000,000 transfer-

or's exemption is allocated to the trust, one-half of the value will be taxable on the child's death. If the trust by that time grows to $3,000,000, the taxable amount will be $1,500,000. If the initial trust had been divided in two, the trustee conceivably could have invested the exempt trust in growth assets and the nonexempt trust in fixed-income nongrowth assets, thereby limiting the latter trust to $1,000,000 on the child's death and having the exempt trust grow to $2,000,000. The taxable amount will then be only $1,000,000, not $1,500,000. Moreover, invasions of principal for the child could have been made entirely from the nonexempt trust, further reducing the taxable amount. Similarly, if a "QTIP" trust (see §4.20) is divided into exempt and nonexempt parts, and the trustee is directed to pay the estate tax chargeable to the "QTIP" trust on the surviving spouse's death out of the nonexempt portion, the result will be favorable because a greater amount will pass free of the generation-skipping transfer tax.

2. If a trust for a child will not be exempt from generation-skipping transfer tax on the child's death, the estate owner should consider giving the child a general power of appointment over such trust. See §2.8. This power will subject the assets to estate tax in the child's estate, but will remove them from the generation-skipping transfer tax. If the child's estate is less than $2,500,000, this result will be advantageous, because the marginal estate tax bracket will be less than 50 per cent, the flat generation-skipping transfer tax rate effective January 1, 1988.

3. If possible, discretionary trusts for children and their issue, where the trustee has authority to sprinkle income to both children and grandchildren (or other issue), should be avoided. (For a discussion of discretionary trusts, see §§5.9 to 5.14.) The reason is that, if distributions are made to the children's issue, the distributed amounts will be treated as taxable distributions. See Supplement §5.39. Where the distributions are of income, they will be subject not only to the generation-skipping transfer tax, but also to the recipient's income tax. If distributions are subject to both taxes, an income tax deduction for the amount of the generation-skipping transfer tax will be allowed (I.R.C. §164(a)(5)). The benefit from this deduction (starting in 1988) will usually not exceed 28 per cent of the generation-skipping transfer tax. Despite whatever benefit there is from the income tax deduction, it would be preferable for the distribution to have been made to the child rather than to the child's issue, because the generation-skipping transfer tax would have been avoided. The child could, if he or she wishes, then gift the distribution to the grandchild.

4.   If nonexempt generation-skipping transfers cannot be avoided, it usually is preferable for the transfer to be first, a taxable termination (see Supplement §5.38); second, a direct skip (see Supplement §5.37); and third, a taxable distribution (see Supplement §5.39). The taxable termination type transfer is the least onerous because the tax is not imposed at the time of the gift or on the death of the transferor, but rather on the child's death. Since the assets are not subject to estate tax in the child's estate, the generation-skipping transfer tax at the time it is paid becomes a real burden only if it is a higher rate than the marginal estate tax bracket would have been in the child's estate. The direct skip causes the generation-skipping transfer tax to be imposed no later than the transferor's death on the amount of the initial principal transferred. The tax must thereby be paid sooner than in a taxable termination or taxable-distribution type transfer, but once the tax is imposed, neither subsequent appreciation of principal nor income distributions are subject to the generation-skipping transfer tax. The direct skip in most cases is less onerous than the taxable-distribution type transfer. Although in the latter transfer, the generation-skipping transfer tax is not imposed until some time after the transfer is made, all income distributions are subject to both the generation-skipping transfer tax and income tax and, moreover, subsequent principal appreciation when distributed is subject to generation-skipping transfer tax.

VI.   Recommended Reading

Insert after Halbach in the recommended reading list on page 100:

Jones, "Ten Per Cent Tables Enhance Community Property Election Will" 13 *Estate Planning* 82 (1986).

Insert after Moore in the recommended reading list on page 100:

Mulligan and Boulton, "New Generation-Skipping Transfer Tax" 14 *Estate Planning* 10 and 66 (1987).

Avoiding Probate

6

I. Probate in General

§6.2   B. What is Subject to Probate?

At the end of the next to last paragraph on page 103, insert:

California law has been amended, effective January 1, 1985, to provide that even separate property passing outright to the surviving spouse need not be probated. Cal Prob Code §649.1(a).

III. Methods of Avoiding Probate

A. Joint Tenancy

2. Tax Characteristics

§6.17   a. Gift Taxes

The seventh sentence of the last paragraph on page 110 is changed to read:

Such presumption can be overcome by evidence proving a common understanding that the character of the property is to be other than joint tenancy, except that a transmutation made after 1985 of joint tenancy property between spouses into another form of ownership is not valid unless made in writing. Cal. Civil Code §5110.730.

c.   Income Taxes

§6.21   i. Income Tax Basis

The seventh sentence of the last paragraph on page 112 is changed to read:

The husband later dies and at the same time the security is worth $25,000.

4.   Dissolving the Joint Tenancy

§6.25   b. Methods of Dissolving the Joint Tenancy

At the end of the text on page 116, add the following citation:

See also Cal Civil Code §683.2.

C.   Disposition By Contract

§6.30   3. Pension and Profit Sharing Plan Benefits

At the end of the text on page 118, add:

The Deficit Reduction Act of 1984 eliminated the estate tax exclusion for death benefits payable under qualified retirement plans. Act §525.

IV.   Recommended Reading

Insert after Holdsworth in the recommended reading list on page 118:

Johnson, "Survivorship Interest With Persons Other Than A Spouse: The Cost of Probate Avoidance" 20 *Real Prop, Prob and Tr J* 985 (1985)

Using a Revocable Living Trust

7

II. Funded Revocable Living Trust

B. Typical Uses

§7.3   1. Probate Avoidance—Consistent with Tax Plan

The first sentence of the third paragraph on page 121 is changed to read:

To carry out the couple's dual objective, which is to avoid probate and to preclude at least a portion of the decedent's interest in the assets from going outright to the surviving spouse and being taxed again upon the surviving spouse's death, the couple should transfer their assets to a funded revocable living trust.

§7.4   2. Lifetime Uses

At the end of the text on page 122, add:

An alternative to the use of a funded revocable living trust to avoid a guardianship or conservatorship of an incompetent estate owner is the use of a general *durable* power of attorney, if permitted by state law. Unlike an ordinary power, a durable power remains effective despite the subsequent incapacity of the principal so that the agent's power to perform acts on behalf of the principal continues even during the time that the principal is incompetent.

Since a durable power is not sanctioned by the general principles of the law of agency, it is effective only in those jurisdictions which enact enabling legislation. Various states have enacted all or portions of the Uniform Durable Power of Attorney Act, which validates the use of a durable power. (For example, see Cal. Civil Code §2400 *et seq*). By using a durable power, an estate owner may designate an agent who will have the power, if and when the estate owner becomes incompetent, to manage the owner's estate without the necessity of court intervention.

C.   During Life of Grantor

§7.6.   1. Expense and Nuisance

Following the eighth line from the top on page 124 add:

The Tax Court has indicated that, although fees and expenses for tax advice and tax planning are deductible, the portion of estate planning fees and costs that the taxpayer incurred to avoid probate are not. *Epp v Commr* 78 TC 801 (1982). Even that portion of the expenses which is otherwise deductible is subject to the 2 per cent floor restriction imposed by the Tax Reform Act of 1986. Under this limitation, only miscellaneous (below the line) deductions which in the aggregate exceed 2 per cent of adjusted gross income may be deducted. I.R.C. §67.

2.   Transfer of Assets

a.   Legal Problems Incident to Transfer of Certain Assets

§7.11   iii. Real Estate

The last three sentences of the last paragraph on page 127 are changed to read:

The Garn-St. Germain Depository Institutions Act of 1982, Pub L. No 97-320, 96 Stat 1469, deals with the validity of such due on transfer clauses. The Act has been interpreted by the Federal Home Loan Bank Board, to whom authority to issue regulations has been delegated, to permit a lender to exercise such a clause even if the transfer is to a revocable trust. 12 C.F.R. §591.5(b)(2)(ii); 48 Fed. Reg. 21,559 (Apr 26, 1983). Only when the transfer is of a residence in which the borrower resides is the right of the lender to accelerate the loan restricted. 12 C.F.R. §591.5(b)(1)(vi).

§7.12   iv. Interest in a Professional Practice

The following sentence is added at the end of the text on page 127:

In the case of a California medical corporation, however, it may be possible to transfer the stock interest to a funded revocable living trust when the licensed physician is the sole trustee of the trust and has the sole beneficial interest in the shares of stock. California Medical Board Legal Opinion 79-5 (Feb 16, 1979).

b.   Tax Problems During the Grantor's Life

§7.16   i. Tax Reporting Requirements

The third sentence of the first paragraph on page 128 is changed to read:

The Regulations now provide that, where the grantor or the grantor's spouse is a trustee or co-trustee, a trust income tax return need not be filed and an employer identification number need not be obtained until the trust becomes irrevocable.

§7.17   ii. Stock in Subchapter S Corporation

The citation at the end of the second to the last sentence on page 128 is changed to read:

I.R.C. §1361(c)(2)(A)(i).

§7.18   iii. Installment Obligations

The reference to I.R.C. §453(b) in the first sentence of the text on page 128 is changed to read:

I.R.C. §453B

§7.20   v. "Flower" Bonds

The second sentence of the last paragraph on page 130 is changed to read:

Moreover, any "flower" bonds in the estate which could have been used to pay an estate tax deficiency, even if not so used but sold after death, must be valued for estate tax purposes at par value.

After §7.21 vi. Combining Community Property and Noncommunity Property Assets on page 130, add new section:

§7.21A   vii. Gifting Assets from the Trust

The Internal Revenue Service has taken the position that gifts made from a revocable trust to third persons within three years before the grantor's death are includable in the grantor's estate under I.R.C. §§2035(d)(2) and 2038. Letter Rul. 8609005. The ruling seems questionable because, if the grantor had retained title to the assets and gifted them directly within three years of death, the three-year rule would not apply. See §2.12. Nevertheless, since the issue has been raised by the Internal Revenue Service, it would be advisable to have the grantor remove assets which he desires to gift from the revocable trust, transfer title to himself, and later gift them directly to the donee.

D.   After Death of Grantor

3.   Tax Considerations

§7.26   b. Loss of Probate Entity as Taxpayer

The following is added at the end of the text on page 134:

The Tax Reform Act of 1986 added two features which are to the advantage of a probate estate as compared to a funded living trust. First, estates may continue to select a fiscal year, but trusts are now required to select a calendar year. I.R.C. §645. A fiscal year can be advantageous in deferring income. See §§15.12 to 15.14. Second, all trusts must now make quarterly estimated payments of income tax, but estates need not do so during the first two taxable years of their existence. I.R.C. §6654(1).

§7.27 c. Estate Tax Exemption for Proceeds of Qualified Retirement Plan Death Benefits

At the end of the text on page 135, add:

The Deficit Reduction Act of 1984 eliminated the estate tax exclusion for death benefits payable under qualified retirement plans. Act §525.

§7.31 g. Stock in Subchapter S Corporation (After Grantor's Death)

The citation at the end of the second sentence of the second paragraph on page 137 is changed to read:

I.R.C. §1361(c)(2)(A)(ii)

The citation at the end of the third sentence of the second paragraph on page 137 is changed to read:

I.R.C. §1361(c)(3)(A)(iii)

The second sentence of the third paragraph (including the citation) on page 137 is changed to read:

Under the Subchapter S Revision Act of 1982, a qualified Subchapter S trust is one that has (1) all of its income distributed to a citizen or resident of the United States; (2) at any given time only one income beneficiary, who, during his or her lifetime, is the exclusive beneficiary insofar as both income and principal distributions are concerned; (3) provided for the termination of the income interest on the earlier of the beneficiary's death or the termination of the trust, and requires that on termination of the trust during the beneficiary's life all the assets of the trust be distributed to such beneficiary; and (4) had the beneficiary make an irrevocable election to be treated as the tax owner of the trust. I.R.C. §1361(d)(3).

IV. Recommended Reading

Insert after Halbach in the recommended reading list on page 143:

Houston, "What Portion of Estate Planning Fees Are Deductible?" 10 *Estate Planning* 66 (1983).

Insert after Uri in the recommended reading list on page 144:

"Estate Planning for Subchapter "S" Shareholder" 17 *Real Prop, Prob and Tr J* 724 (1982).

Making Gifts

8

---

§8.1   I. General Considerations in Making Gifts

In the last sentence of the last paragraph, change the citation casename of "Deidrick v Commr" to:

Diedrich v Commr

At the end of the last paragraph on page 147 add:

The Supreme Court in *Diedrich v Commr* 457 US 191 (1982) resolved the question by holding that when the gift tax paid by the donee exceeds the donor's adjusted basis in the gifted asset, the excess is taxable gain to the donor. To illustrate, assume A owns an asset worth $1,000,000 with an income tax basis of $50,000. He gifts the asset to B, upon condition that B pay the gift tax of $200,000. A will have a taxable gain of $150,000. Section 1026 of the Deficit Reduction Act of 1984 provides that the *Diedrich* decision is not retroactive to net gifts made before March 4, 1981, Pub L No 98-369.

A.   Tax Advantages

1.   To Reduce Estate Taxes

d.   Gifts Included in Gross Estate

§8.7   i. Gifts Made within Three Years of Death

At the end of the first paragraph on page 150 add:

The Technical Corrections Act of 1982 makes it clear that all gifts of life insurance, as well as I.R.C. §§2036, 2037, and 2038 transfers, but *not* exercises of general powers of appointment under I.R.C. §2041, are included in the gross estate even when a gift tax return was not required to be filed. I.R.C. §2035(d)(2).

§8.9   2. To Reduce Income Taxes

The first paragraph on page 151 is changed to read:

Another important tax reason for making gifts is to reduce the income taxes payable on the income earned by the gifted assets. This may be illustrated by an example. Assume an estate owner owns $300,000 of securities which earn $15,000 per year. He is in a 28 per cent income tax bracket and hence his net after-tax yield is $10,800. If he gifts these securities to his son, who is only in a 15 per cent bracket, the son's after-tax yield from the securities will be $12,750 per year. If, however, the son is under age 14, the son's unearned income in excess of $500 will be taxed at the father's marginal rate of 28 per cent. For a further discussion of the so-called "Kiddie Tax," see Supplement §8.18. Additionally, regardless of whether or not income taxes will be saved, the donor, by making the gift, will prevent his estate from being increased by the income from the gifted asset. Therefore, his estate tax will tend to be less than if he had not made the gift.

III. To Whom Should the Gift Be Made

A. Spouse

§8.14 1. Gift Tax Avoidance

At the end of the first paragraph on page 153, add:

The estate planner should counsel the estate owner to consider whether the marriage is a stable one before making any gifts to the other spouse.

The second full sentence on page 154 is changed to read:

A qualifying terminable interest requires that the donee spouse be entitled to receive all the income from the property at least annually and that no person be able to appoint the property during the spouse's lifetime to anyone other than the spouse.

B. Children

§8.18 2. Income Tax Savings

The entire section is changed to read:

As compared to interspousal gifts, gifts to children may frequently be used to advantage in saving income taxes. This may be illustrated by an example. Assume that the estate owner and his spouse have securities worth $180,000 which earn $7,200 per year. If they are in a 28 per cent bracket, the taxes on such income will be $2,016 per year. If they gave these securities in equal shares to three children, each child would have income of $2,400 per year, which, if the child is not under age 14, would result in little or no income tax.

If a child is under age 14, the income from the gift received by that child may be taxed at a higher rate. Under the Tax Reform Act of 1986, the unearned income of a minor under age 14 which exceeds $500 (plus another $500, or a total of $1,000, if the minor allocates $500 of his standard deduction to unearned income) will, if at least one of the minor's parents is living, be taxed at the greater of the parents' or the minor's marginal rate. I.R.C. § 1(i). This rule applies to all unearned income of a minor under age 14, regardless of its source, and not merely to unearned income resulting from gifts from the parent to the minor. Accordingly, in the above example, if one of the children is under the age of 14, that child's share of the income will be taxed at 28 per cent rather than at 15 per cent.

Even if a child is over age 14, but is claimed as a dependent on the parents' return, the personal exemption may not be taken on the child's return (I.R.C. §151(d)(2)) and only $500 of the child's standard deduction may be used to offset the child's unearned income. I.R.C. §63(c)(5).

§8.19 3. Problems in Making Gifts to Children

Delete the last sentence in the text on page 156 and insert:

For the effect of the generation-skipping transfer tax, see Supplement §§5.34 to 5.42.

C. Grandchildren

§8.20 1. Avoiding the Generation-Skipping Transfer Tax

At the end of the text on page 157, add:

The Tax Reform Act of 1986 significantly altered the generation-skipping transfer tax. For a full discussion, see Supplement §§5.34 to 5.42.

§8.21 2. Income Tax Savings

At the end of the text on page 157, add:

For the effect of the "Kiddie Tax" on minors under age 14, see Supplement §8.18; for the effect of the generation-skipping transfer tax, see Supplement §§5.34 to 5.42.

IV. Selection of Assets to Give

§8.23 B. Tax Rules to Follow in Gifting Assets

At the end of item 5 on page 160 add:

There is also another income tax problem when the amount of the encumbrance (whether or not the donor has personal liability) on the gifted property exceeds the property's adjusted basis. The donor, by making the gift, will realize taxable income on the amount of the excess. Reg. §1.1001-2(B)(4)(iii); see *Estate of Levine v Commr* 634 F2d 12 (2d Cir 1980).

The last three lines of item 6 on page 160 are deleted.

The citation at the end of item 7 on page 160 is changed to read:

See I.R.C. §453B.

The second sentence (including the citation) in item 8 on page 160 is changed to read:

The corporation's election not to be taxed as a regular corporation will automatically be revoked whenever such a trust becomes a shareholder, unless such trust is a "qualified Subchapter S trust." I.R.C. §1361(b)(1)(B) and (c)(2).

V. Manner of Making Gifts

B. Gifts Under Custodian Statute

§8.28 1. Legal Requirements

At the end of the last paragraph on page 162 add:

California adopted a variation of the Uniform Transfers to Minors Act in place of the Uniform Gifts to Minors Act. Cal Prob Code §3900 *et seq.* Under California law, assets of any type may now be held by the custodian. Moreover, the donor may, by a specific statement in the document of inter vivos transfer, delay the termination of the custodianship until age 21. For the effect of the Uniform Transfers to Minors Act on testamentary gifts, see supplement §3.20.

2. Tax Consequences

§8.31 c. Estate Tax

The second sentence on page 163 is changed to read:

The power of the custodian, under the Uniform Act, to transfer all of the custodial assets to the minor before the minor reaches age 18 is considered to be a power to terminate the custodianship.

C. Gifts in Trust

3.   Gift Tax

§8.34   a. $10,000 Annual Exclusion

At the end of the second paragraph on page 164 add:

Because of new valuation tables (see Appendix VIII of the Supplement for an explanation), new calculations should be substituted in the example in the text. At age 50, whether A is a male or a female, 84.743 per cent of the gift, or $84,743, will be considered the value of the income interest.

§8.35   b. Crummey Trust

At the end of the second sentence of the first paragraph on page 165 insert:

The beneficiary's withdrawal right may extend into the next calendar year without negating the validity of the *Crummey* power. Rev. Rul. 83-108, I.R.B. 1983-30, 14.

The following sentence is inserted prior to the last sentence of the third paragraph on page 165:

However, if the beneficiary holds several $5,000 or 5 per cent powers (either in the same trust or in different trusts), he or she is not entitled to more than one five-and-five exemption in any one calendar year. Rev. Rul. 85-88, I.R.B. 1985-26.

At the end of the text on page 165 add:

Another way to solve the gift tax problem, when the amount of the lapse will exceed the *five-and-five power,* is by giving the beneficiary a *hanging* power. A hanging power is one which, unless otherwise limited, does not lapse if it is not exercised, but continues into future years until it is exercised. When a hanging power is combined with a provision that each year the power is still in existence it will lapse if not exercised, up to $5,000 or 5 per cent of the principal, whichever is greater, it could be a valuable device. For example, if the donor establishes a trust for the benefit of one beneficiary who is given a *Crummey* hanging power and the donor contributes $100,000 in one year to the trust, only the beneficiary's right to withdraw $5,000 will lapse if he or she fails to exercise the power. The right to withdraw the remaining $5,000 of the available annual gift tax exclusion would be suspended and yet the full $10,000 annual gift tax exclusion would be allowed. In the following year, assuming no further gifts were made to the trust, the beneficiary would still have the right to withdraw the nonlapsed, unwithdrawn $5,000 and, if he or she should not choose to withdraw, the lapse will be protected from gift tax by the five-and-five exception. Upon the beneficiary's death, any unexercised and nonlapsed power will be taxable in his or her estate.

§8.36 c. Minor's Trust

At the end of the last paragraph on page 166, add:

For circumstances where the income will be taxed to the parent of the minor, see §§8.42, 8.43 and 9.13, or at the parent's marginal rate, see Supplement §8.18.

5. Income Tax

§8.39 a. Avoiding Income Being Taxable to Grantor

The sections referred to at the end of Items 2, 3 and 4 in the first paragraph on page 169 should read: §8.40, §8.41 and §8.42.

The last paragraph on page 169 is deleted and the following inserted in place thereof:

The Tax Reform Act of 1986 provides that, if a grantor's spouse is living with the grantor, any power held by the spouse shall be deemed to be held by the grantor. I.R.C. §672(e).

§8.40 i. Retention of Powers Affecting Beneficial Enjoyment

At the end of the text on page 170, add:

The Tax Reform Act of 1986 provides that, if a grantor's spouse is

living with the grantor, any power held by the spouse shall be deemed
to be held by the grantor. I.R.C. §672(e).

§8.41   ii. Administrative Powers

*At the end of the second sentence of item 2 on page 171, insert the
following sentence:*

In this context, "the beginning of the taxable year" means the year in
which the loan was made, not the beginning of the following year.
Accordingly, any borrowing by the grantor, even if repaid within the
same year, will cause the income of the trust to be taxable to him. Rev.
Rul. 86-82, 1986-1 C.B. 253.

At the end of the text on page 171, add:

The Tax Reform Act of 1986 provides that, if a grantor's spouse is
living with the grantor, any power held by the spouse shall be deemed
to be held by the grantor. I.R.C. §672(e).

§8.42   iii. Income Held for Future Use of the
           Grantor

At the end of the text on page 171, add:

For a discussion of what constitutes support of children, see §9.13.
The Tax Reform Act of 1986 provides that, if a grantor's spouse is
living with the grantor, any power held by the spouse shall be deemed
to be held by the grantor. I.R.C. §672(e).

§8.43   b. Avoiding Income Being Taxable to
           Persons Other Than Grantor or
           Beneficiary

At the end of the text on page 172, add:

For a discussion of what constitutes support, see §9.13.

c. Normal Rules of Trust Income Taxation

§8.44 i. The Extent to which Income Is Taxable to the Trust and to the Beneficiary

At the end of the text on page 173 add:

By having the estate owner create more than one discretionary trust for the same beneficiary, an income tax saving may result. Splitting the income among various trusts that accumulate income will usually result in a lower total tax than would have been the case with a single trust. New I.R.C. §643(e) provides, however, that multiple trusts are to be treated as a single trust if they have (1) the same grantor and substantially the same primary beneficiary, and (2) an avoidance of income tax as their principal purpose. A husband and wife are to be treated as one person.

The Tax Reform Act of 1986 requires trusts to select a calendar year. I.R.C. §645. Hence, deferring the taxation of income to the beneficiary by the use of the trust fiscal year will no longer be possible.

§8.46 d. Sale by Trust Within Two Years

At the end of the text on page 175, add:

The Tax Reform Act of 1986 provides that long-term capital gains are to be taxed at a rate not in excess of 28 per cent. I.R.C. §1(j). However, for years after 1987, the inclusion of capital gains in income may cause certain of the taxpayer's income to be taxed at the 33 per cent bracket.

VI. Alternatives to Gifts

§8.48 B. Sale of a Remainder Interest

At the end of the second paragraph on page 176 add:

The Internal Revenue Service has issued Private Letter Rulings which concede that adequate and full consideration means an amount equal to the value of the remainder interest. Letter Ruls. 7806001 and 8145012. See, however, *Gradow v US* 87-1 USTC ¶13,711 (Ct Cl 1987). This case, in the context of a forced widow's election, defines *full consideration* to mean the full value of the transferred property and not just the full value of the remainder interest. (See Supplement §5.24.) The rationale of the case appears to be limited to the situation where the sale of the remainder interest arises out of an election under a will or a trust taking effect after death. It is to be hoped that the decision will not be applied in the nontestamentary sale of a remainder interest discussed here.

At the end of the text on page 177 add new paragraphs:

Because of new valuation tables (see Appendix VIII of the Supplement for an explanation), new calculations should be substituted in the example in the text. Accordingly, in the fourth paragraph, the value of the remainder interest, at age 55, is 19.954 per cent of the total value of the property. (See Supplement Appendix VIII, Table A.) The estate owner could sell the asset worth $1,000,000 for $199,540, which would be adequate and full consideration thereof, and his or her estate would be reduced by $800,460, instead of $617,760, as stated in the text.

A somewhat different use of a life estate-remainder device can also eliminate an asset from one's estate. Rather than have the estate owner sell a remainder interest in an asset which he or she already owns to a family member, the asset may be purchased by the estate owner and a younger family member from a third party. The estate owner will purchase the life estate and the younger family member, the remainder interest. Each will pay his or her actuarial portion of the consideration. Under the facts of the above example, the estate owner (age 55) would pay $800,460 and the younger family member, $199,540. When the estate owner dies, nothing will be included in the estate because the life estate terminates. Since the terminated life estate was not a retained one, I.R.C. §2036(a), the question of what constitutes adequate and full consideration, discussed above, is not applicable.

A potentially serious problem exists if the remainder interest transaction is structured as a trust, rather than as a legal life estate-remainder interest relationship. The trust may be held to be an association taxable as a corporation. I.R.C. §7701(a)(3); *Morrisey v Commr* 296 US 344 (1935). In that event, earnings of the trust will be subject to corporate income tax and distributions from the trust, to the extent of the trust's earnings, will be taxable to the recipient as a dividend. A preferable method of structuring the transaction would be to create a legal life estate-remainderman relationship and to define each party's rights and duties in a written agreement.

§8.49   C. Grantor Annuity

At the end of the last paragraph on page 178 add:

In the situation where the donor transfers noncash assets to the trust, it is arguable that a private annuity sale was made and that the transferred property is not includable in the donor's estate. See Supplement §11.13.

Because of new valuation tables (see Appendix VIII of the Supplement for an explanation), new calculations should be substituted in the example in the text. The new tables are predicated on a 10 per cent interest factor. Accordingly, a grantor annuity has lost some of its appeal. In the example in the text, the value of the father's annuity would be only $85,241 ($12,000 times 7.1034, see Supplement Appendix VIII, Table B). As a result, the father would be making a gift of $14,759 ($100,000 minus $85,241). In order to avoid having any part of the transfer constitute a gift, the grantor would have to receive the 12 per cent payout for at least 19 years, instead of 13 years as illustrated in the text.

§8.50   D. Grantor Income Trust (New)

The 1983 amendment to the regulations replacing the 6 per cent interest factor valuation tables with the 10 per cent interest factor valuation tables (see Supplement Appendix VIII) has given rise to a variation of the grantor annuity device discussed in §8.49. The variation is called a grantor income trust. In most situations its use will be preferable to that of a grantor annuity.

Under the grantor income trust device, the donor transfers assets to an irrevocable trust which provides for the income (rather than a specified rate of return) to be paid to the donor for a fixed period of time. At the end of that period, the trust terminates and the trust assets are distributed to the remaindermen donees. The gift of the remainder interest is deemed to be completed at the time the gift is made. T.A.M. 8546001. The value of the gift is computed by referring to the valuation tables set forth in Reg. §25.2512–5 (see Supplement Appendix VIII, Table B).

To illustrate, assume that a parent, age 55, transfers an asset worth $500,000 to a grantor income trust. He hopes that he will live past age 70, but when he reaches that age he anticipates that he will no longer need the income from, or the use of, the asset. Therefore, the trust provides that he is to receive the income (or, if the transferred asset is a residence, the use of the residence) for 15 years, at which time the principal is to go to his children. By setting up the trust, he is making a taxable gift of only the remainder interest, which, according to the Treasury Department tables (see Supplement Appendix VIII, Table B), is worth $119,196 ($500,000 times .238392). This gift will normally not cause a gift tax, unless the donor's unified credit has been completely used for previous gifts. The donor will have eliminated the excess of the value of the asset at the time of his death over the amount of the gift from his taxable estate. If the asset value does not change, he will have eliminated $380,804 ($500,000 minus $119,196).

The success of the plan depends on the donor, in the example, outliving the 15-year period. If the donor should die in the meantime, the value of the asset at the time of death will be included in the estate under I.R.C. §2036. (See §2.14.) Elderly persons may therefore wish to shorten the period during which the income is retained, while young persons can make the period longer. The longer the period, the smaller the value of the gift, which, in effect, results in a greater exclusion from the estate. By the same token, when a longer period is selected, the donor has a greater chance of dying before the trust terminates. The duration of the trust must therefore be determined very carefully.

In many cases it will be advisable for the trust to provide that if, in fact, the donor dies prior to the expiration of the income interest, the trust assets will be distributed to his or her estate. This provision will further reduce the value of the gift by the actuarial possibility that the donor may die while still entitled to receive the income from the trust. See T.A.M. 8546001. For example, if this provision were included in the 15-year grantor income trust for the 55-year-old donor described above, the value of the gift would be $87,172 (see Table LN of Paragraph (f) of Reg. §20.2031-7) instead of $119,196. If the donor outlives the 15-year period and the asset value does not change, he or she will have eliminated $412,828 ($500,000 minus $87,172) from the estate, rather than $380,804.

VII.   Recommended Reading

Insert before Bolmuth in the recommended reading list on page 178:

Adams and Bieber, "Making '5 and 5' Equal 20: *Crummey* Powers After ERTA" 122 No 9 *Trusts and Estates* 22 (1983).

Blake and Pearle, "College Education May Be a Parent's Support Obligation" 11 *Estate Planning* 322 (1984).

Insert after Costello in the recommended reading list on page 178:

Dye, "I.R.S. Income Tax Roadblock to Use of *Crummey* Provisions" 10 *Estate Planning* 220 (1983).

Early, "Income Taxation of Lapsed Powers of Withdrawal" 62 *Journal of Taxation* 198 (1985).

Insert after Flannery in the recommended reading list on page 178:

Gilbert, "Selling a Remainder Interest for a Private Annuity" 124 No 12 *Trusts and Estates* 10 (1985).

Insert after Horvitz in the recommended reading list on page 178:

Mahon, "Grantor Lead Trusts" 123 No 8 *Trusts and Estates* 26 (1984).

Insert after Weinstock in the recommended reading list on page 178:

Weinstock, "Private Lead Trusts and Life Estate-Remainder Interest Purchases" 1983 *UCLA Estate Planning Institute* 409.

Using a Short-Term Trust

9

The following material pertains to the entire Chapter 9 of the text:

The use of a traditional 10-year short-term trust to shift income to another person was effectively eliminated by the Tax Reform Act of 1986 (the act) which repealed the 10-year reversionary interest rule. See §9.5; I.R.C. §673. Moreover, the use of a spousal remainder trust (see Supplement §9.22) was also eliminated. The act provides that, if a grantor's spouse is living with the grantor, any power or interest held by the spouse shall be treated as if held by the grantor. I.R.C. §672(e).

A reversionary interest trust may still be used to shift income away from the grantor, if the value of the reversionary interest does not exceed 5 per cent of the value of the assets transferred to the trust. I.R.C. §673(a). Various ways may be considered by the estate planner to so limit the value of the reversionary interest. Some suggestions are:

1. Have the trust provide that the beneficiary receive a yearly annuity amount which actuarially will be worth at least 95 per cent of the value of the principal transferred to the trust. Under the valuation tables (see Table B contained in Appendix VIII of the Supplement), the value of a 15.5 per cent annuity for 10 years would be worth over 95 per cent. Hence, if the grantor transfers $100,000 to a trust, which provides that the child receive $15,500 per year for 10 years, with the reversion to the grantor, the income earned by the trust would not be taxed to the grantor. At the present rates of return on investments, however, it would be very difficult for the trust to actually earn 15.5 per cent, so that substantial amounts of principal would have to be used to satisfy the annuity payments.

2. Similarly, the beneficiary of a 10-year trust could be given the right to all of the income, plus a power to invade 5 per cent of

the principal each year. This right and power will cause the reversionary interest to be worth less than 5 per cent.

3. An independent person may be given an unlimited discretionary power to invade principal for the benefit of the beneficiary during the term of the trust. This power eliminates any value which the reversionary interest may otherwise have.

Carrying out any of these suggestions will cause a taxable gift of the nonreversionary interest, which will be worth at least 95 per cent of the value of the assets transferred to the trust. In the formerly useful traditional 10-year short-term trust, the value of a taxable gift was only 61.4457 per cent (see Supplement §9.10). Consideration should be given to whether the income tax savings are worth the increased transfer tax cost.

III. Tax Rules

A. Income Taxes

5. Capital Gain Problem

§9.9 b. Possible Solutions

The first two sentences of the third paragraph on page 184 are changed to read:

Another problem with allocating gains to income arises when appreciated assets are transferred to a short-term trust and capital gains are allocated in the trust instrument to the income beneficiary. Where the grantor is not the trustee, the Internal Revenue Service has indicated that there is an immediate taxable gift of the amount of the unrealized appreciation.

The fourth sentence of the third paragraph on page 184 is changed to read:

There will be a taxable gift by the grantor at the time of the transfer to the trust not only of the income interest in $70,000 (see §9.10), but also of the total unrealized appreciation of $20,000.

§9.10   B. Gift Taxes

At the end of the first paragraph on page 185, insert the following paragraphs:

It usually is not advisable to obtain the annual exclusion by means of a *Crummey* power (see §8.35). By including such a power, the grantor is gifting not only the income interest, but also a portion of the principal. Moreover, if the beneficiary permits the power to lapse and the lapsed amount exceeds $5,000 or 5 per cent of the principal, whichever is greater, the beneficiary will be deemed to have made a taxable gift back to the grantor.

The value of the gifted income interest may be reduced by providing for a portion of the income to be paid to the grantor. For example, if the trust provided that an amount equal to 10 per cent of the value of the assets contributed to the trust be paid annually to the grantor and any remaining income be paid to the children, the value of the gift to the children would be zero. See Reg. §25.2512-5. (See Supplement Appendix, Table VIII B).

At the end of the text on page 185 add:

Because of new valuation tables (see Appendix VIII of the Supplement for an explanation), new calculations should be substituted in the example in the text. In the example, if a transfer is made to a short-term trust for a period of 10 years, 61.4457 per cent (see Supplement Appendix VIII, Table B), rather than 44.1605 per cent, of the fair market value of the transferred assets will be the value of the income interest. By reason of the $10,000 annual exclusion, $16,275, rather than $22,644, may be contributed to a 10-year trust without causing the gift to be taxable.

§9.11   C. Estate Taxes

At the end of the text on page 186 add:

Because of new valuation tables (see Appendix VIII of the Supplement for an explanation), new calculations should be substituted in the example in the text. The reference to 83.9619 per cent in the fourth sentence should be changed to 75.1315 per cent. See Supplement Appendix VIII, Table B.

§9.12 IV. Considerations in Deciding Whether a Short-Term Trust Is Appropriate

At the end of the second paragraph on page 186 add:

Because of new valuation tables (see Appendix VIII of the Supplement for an explanation), new calculations should be substituted in the example in the text. In the example, the value of the income interest will now be $61,446 ($100,000 times 61.445 per cent, see Supplement Appendix VIII, Table B). $161,446, rather than $144,161, will, in effect, be taxed for estate tax purposes.

V. Specific Uses

§9.13 A. For Children

At the end of the fifth sentence of the first paragraph on page 187 insert:

But see *Frederick C Braun, Jr* 48 TCM 210 (1984), holding that, under New Jersey law, expenditures for private school constitute support payments.

At the end of the first sentence of the third paragraph on page 187, insert:

But see *Frederick C Braun, Jr* 48 TCM 210 (1984), holding that, under New Jersey law, a financially capable parent has a legal duty to contribute to the college or postgraduate study of adult children who are qualified students. Under California statutory law, a parent has no legal duty to support or educate a child over the age of 18, unless the child is under the age of 19, is a full-time high school student, and resides with one of the parents. Cal. Civil Code §196.5.

§9.17 E. Leaseback of Assets

After the Quinlivan case in the second to last sentence of the second paragraph on page 190 add:

; *Rosenfeld v Commr* 706 F2d 1277 (2d Cir 1983).

VI.   Selecting Assets to Transfer to Short-Term Trust

§9.19   B. Transferring a Partnership or Other Business Interest

The citation at the end of the second paragraph on page 190 should be changed to read:

I.R.C. §1361(b)(1)(B), (c)(2) and (d).

After B. Transferring a Partnership or Other Business Interest on page 190 add new section:

§9.19A   C. Funding the Trust with Borrowed Funds (New)

An estate owner may be in a high income tax bracket, but may lack sufficient assets to fund a short-term trust that would shift income to a lower bracket family member. Although the device has been attempted, it is clear that the trust cannot be initially funded with the estate owner's interest-bearing note. The interest will not be deductible to the donor on the ground that no consideration was given for the note. See *Brown v Commr* 241 F2d 827 (8th Cir 1957); *Linder v Commr* 68 TC 792 (1977). The result would be the same even if the donor secured the note with collateral. *Strimling v Commr* 46 TCM 211 (1983) affd 734 F2d 1377 (9th Cir 1984).

The above device may be varied somewhat and may then succeed. The donor should first borrow funds from a bank or other third party and then gift these funds to a short-term trust. After the funds have been held by the trustee for a reasonable period of time, the donor will borrow back monies from the trust to enable him or her to pay the bank loan. For this arrangement to succeed, there must be, at the very least, an independent trustee and, further, the loan from the short-term trust to the donor must provide for adequate interest and security. See I.R.C. §675(3); §9.46. To strengthen the possibility of success, the trustee, while the funds are in the trust, should explore alternate investments. Even if these requirements are met, great care should be taken to avoid any prearranged commitment on the part of the trustee to make a loan to the donor. If there is such a commitment, the Internal Revenue Service will again disregard the donor's note to the trust and deny the interest deduction. See *Johnson v Commr* 86 F2d 712 (2d Cir 1936).

The Tax Reform Act of 1986 phases out the deductibility of personal interest and limits the deductibility of investment interest. I.R.C. §163.

Hence, the ability of the grantor to deduct the interest payments will in any event be restricted.

VII. Alternatives to Using a Short-Term Trust

§9.20 A. Municipal Bonds

At the end of the first paragraph on page 191, insert:

The Tax Reform Act of 1986 provides that the interest from certain municipal bonds, which are considered nonessential function bonds, generally issued after August 7, 1986, is a tax preference item. Therefore, such interest, while not taxable income, may give rise to the alternative minimum tax. I.R.C. §57(a).

§9.21 B. Interest-Free Loan

At the end of the third paragraph on page 192 add:

The Supreme Court in *Dickman v Commr* 465 US 330 (1984) (84-1 USTC ¶13,560) held, contrary to the *Crown* case, that even an interest-free *demand* loan gives rise to a taxable gift. Hence the position of the Internal Revenue Service has been sustained. In the *Dickman* case, the reasonable annual rate of interest was deemed to be the same interest rate as the rate used by the Internal Revenue Service on tax deficiencies and overpayments. See I.R.C. §6621; Supplement §12.52.

The *Dickman* case, by itself, does not eliminate interest-free loans as a viable tool to shift income to a lower bracket taxpayer. It merely imposes a transfer tax when the reasonable value of the interest exceeds the $10,000 annual gift tax exclusion.

The enactment in 1984 of I.R.C. §7872 severely restricts the usefulness of interest-free loans as an alternative to short-term trusts. With certain relatively minor exceptions, the foregone interest, consistent with the *Dickman* decision, is treated as a gift from the lender to the borrower. Similarly, for income tax purposes, an interest-free loan, with minor exceptions, is treated as if the borrower actually paid interest to the lender at a rate based on the market interest rate for federal obligations. Thus, interest income is imputed to the lender and the borrower is given a deductible interest payment based on the federal obligation rate.

§9.22   C. Spousal Remainder Trust (New)

For a married estate owner who desires to shift income to a lower bracket taxpayer donee, but who does not desire to give up the income from his or her assets to this taxpayer for as long as 10 years, the use of what might be called a spousal remainder trust should be explored. Under this device, rather than retaining a reversionary interest, the estate owner can designate his or her spouse as the one to receive the trust remainder at the expiration of the income interest. In this way, the 10-year reversionary requirement (see §9.5) is avoided and the trust period may be much shorter, perhaps even as short as two or three years.

The donor, by giving the remainder interest to his or her spouse, will be making a gift of the remainder interest. This gift can be designed to qualify for the gift tax marital deduction and therefore not be taxable. This may be accomplished by providing that the spouse's remainder interest is vested and that if the spouse is not living upon the termination of the income interest, the remainder interest will be paid to the spouse's estate. See Reg. §25.2523(a)-1(d).

The assets transferred to the spousal remainder trust should consist entirely of the donor's separate property. If community property assets are contributed, the 10-year reversionary rule will continue to apply to the spouse's one-half community property interest, because such one-half interest will revert within 10 years to a grantor of the trust. When the estate of the couple consists of community property, one spouse can gift his or her share of certain assets to the other without gift taxability. I.R.C. §2523(a). It can be anticipated that if this gift and the transfer by the donee spouse to the spousal remainder trust are closely related in time or are part of a prearranged plan, the Internal Revenue Service will argue that the spouse is, in reality, a grantor of the trust. This pitfall can be avoided by dividing certain community property assets so that one-half belongs to each spouse as his or her separate property, and ensuring that only the donor-spouse's one-half is then contributed to the trust.

VIII.   Recommended Reading

Insert after Berall in the recommended reading list on page 192:

Blake and Pearle, "College Education May Be a Parent's Support Obligation" 11 *Estate Planning* 322 (1984).

Insert after Costello and Klepetko in the recommended reading list on page 192:

Edwards, "Interest-Free Loans" 58 *Journal of Taxation* 110 (1983).

Insert after Rossbach in the recommended reading list on page 193:

Simmons, "How the Proper Use of Gift and Borrowback Techniques May Make Children's Educational Expenses Deductible" 64 *Taxes* 110 (1984).

Smith, "The Spousal Remainder Trust" 123 No 4 *Trusts and Estates* 32 (1984).

Life Insurance

10

§10.6 II. Types of Life Insurance Policies

At the end of the text on page 197, add:

In addition to these four basic forms, two relatively new types of insurance are currently being used, namely, universal life and joint life policies. See Supplement §10.59 for a discussion of universal life insurance and §10.44 for a description of joint life insurance.

III. Death Taxation

C. Gift Made within Three Years of Death

§10.14 1. Transfer of Policy within Three Years of Death

At the end of the second paragraph on page 200 add:

But see *Hope v US* 691 F2d 786 (5th Cir 1982) (82-2 USTC ¶13,504) which held that when the insured contributed monies to an insurance trust that paid the premiums, the proceeds were not includable in the insured's estate unless the trustee acted as the insured's agent in purchasing the policies. See also *Estate of Clay* 86 TC 1266 (1986). However, where the trustee paid the premium for the policy with funds gifted by the decedent-insured to the trust as its sole asset, the Tax Court held that the trustee was the agent of the insured. *Estate of Kurihara v Commr* 82 TC 51 No 4 (1984).

V. Income Taxation

§10.21 A. General Rule of Excludability

At the end of the text on page 203, add:

See also Supplement §10.59 for a discussion of the guidelines included in the Deficit Reduction Act of 1984 that apply to investment-oriented life insurance policies, such as universal life insurance and certain endowment policies. These guidelines must be satisfied in order to have the entire proceeds excluded from gross income. If the tests are not met, then only the excess of the face amount of the policy over the net surrender value will be excluded. I.R.C. §7702(g).

§10.22 B. Transfer for Value Rule

At the end of the first paragraph on page 204, add:

Accordingly, where one spouse sells the policy to the other, the transfer for value rule will not apply because even a sale from one spouse to the other is treated as a gift. I.R.C. §10.41(b).

C. Settlement Options

§10.28 5. Interest Portion

At the end of the text on page 205, add the following:

The interest exclusion for the surviving spouse was repealed by the 1986 Tax Reform Act with respect to amounts received in connection with deaths occurring after October 22, 1986.

§10.29 D. Policy Loans and the Interest Deduction

The following paragraph is added at the end of the text on page 207:

The 1986 Tax Reform Act of 1986 amended I.R.C. §163 to provide that personal interest will no longer be deductible by an individual. See I.R.C. §163(h). The loss of this deduction is phased in between 1987 and 1990, so that only the following portion of policy loan interest, otherwise deductible, will be allowable to the taxpayer: 65 per cent in 1987; 40 per cent in 1988; 20 per cent in 1989; and 10 per cent in 1990.

After 1990, no portion of the interest incurred in connection with a life insurance policy loan will be deductible. See I.R.C. §163(h).

VII.   Who Should be Made the Owner?

A.   Wife Ownership

1.   Who Should be the Beneficiary of the Wife-Owned Policy?

§10.40   a. Possibility of Gift Tax to Wife

The first sentence of the third paragraph on page 214 is changed to read:

The more usual way to avoid this taxable gift is to have all of the proceeds of the policy payable to the "A" (marital) trust, provided the wife has a general (see §4.14) or a limited power of appointment (see §4.21) in this trust.

§10.41   b. Possible Taxation in Husband's Estate

At the end of the first paragraph on page 215 add:

The Internal Revenue Service has conceded that, unless the insured is the grantor of the trust, the proceeds will not be included in the insured's estate merely because he or she is the trustee, as long as he or she is not also a beneficiary of the trust. See Rev. Rul. 84-179, 1984-2 CB 195.

§10.42   2. Who Should Get The Policy if the Wife Predeceases the Husband?

Following the citation, just prior to the last sentence of the first paragraph on page 216, insert:

But see Rev. Rul. 84-179, 1984-2 C.B. 195 (which is discussed in supplement §10.41).

§10.43   3. Simultaneous Death

At the end of the text on page 217 add:

In a recent decision the Tax Court held that where the wife owns a life insurance policy on the husband's life, of which the "B" trust is the beneficiary, and the husband and wife die simultaneously, the wife is deemed to be the survivor. Hence, she is deemed to have made a taxable gift to the "B" trust of the *proceeds* of the policy. *Estate of Goldstone v Commr* 78 TC 1143 (1982). The rationale behind the court's decision is that the Uniform Simultaneous Death Act presumes the insured to be the survivor only if the *beneficiary* and the insured die simultaneously. However, where the beneficiary is a nonowner third party (such as the "B" trust), then the owner of the policy is deemed to have survived the insured.

B.   Ownership by Children or Irrevocable Life Insurance Trust

2.   Ownership by Irrevocable Insurance Trust

a.   General Tax Consequences

§10.47   i. Gift Taxes

In the second to the last line of the second paragraph on page 219 delete:

"Letter Rul. 7947008"

At the end of the second paragraph on page 219 add:

The Internal Revenue Service indicated that, pending a further study of the matter, it will not issue advance rulings on whether a *Crummey* power in a life insurance trust qualifies for the present interest exclusion when the income is taxable to the grantor. Rev. Proc. 83-22, 1983-1 C.B. 680.

§10.48   ii. Income Taxes

After item 4 on page 220, add:

5. Giving the grantor, in a nonfiduciary capacity, the power to reacquire the trust corpus by substituting other assets of an equivalent value (Reg. §1.675-1(b)(iii)). See *Estate of Jordah* 65 TC 92 (1975) acq 1977-1 C.B. 1, holding that the trust assets will not be includible in the grantor's estate under I.R.C. §2038(a)(2).

The citation in the second sentence of the fourth paragraph on page 220, of Rev. Proc. 81-37 is changed to read:

Rev. Proc. 81-37, 1981-2 C.B. 592

At the end of the text on page 220, add the following paragraph:

As a result of the enactment of the 1986 Tax Reform Act, no interest deductions in connection with policy loans will be allowed after 1990. (See Supplement §10.29.) Because of the potential risk of having insurance policy proceeds included in the taxable estate because of improperly drafted "defective" trust provisions, it is probably not advisable to use the defective grantor trust technique in a post-1986 Tax Reform Act irrevocable life insurance trust.

§10.50   b. Who Should be the Beneficiaries of the Irrevocable Life Insurance Trust?

At the end of the text on page 222 add:

The Tax Court has held, however, that the husband may be the income beneficiary of the wife's trust when she holds a special power of appointment over the principal of his trust, but he was not given a similar power over the principal of her trust. *Estate of Levy v Commr* TC Memo 1983-453.

In considering who should be the beneficiary of a life insurance trust, one should not overlook the potential generation-skipping transfer tax consequences. See Supplement §§5.34 to 5.42.

IX. Business Life Insurance

§10.53   A. Use in Buy-Sell Agreements

At the end of the third paragraph on page 223, insert the following:

For the possible alternative minimum tax consequences of a corporation owning a life insurance policy, see Supplement §12.14.

§10.54   B. Use in Employee Agreements

At the end of the text on page 224, add the following:

For the possible alternative minimum tax consequences of a corporation owning a life insurance policy, see Supplement §12.14.

§10.55   C. Key Person Life Insurance

At the end of the text on page 225, add the following:

For the possible alternative minimum tax consequences of a corporation owning a life insurance policy, see Supplement §12.14.

X. Use of Life Insurance in Connection with Employee Fringe Benefits

§10.56   A. Group Life Insurance

At the end of the citation following the first sentence in the third paragraph on page 225 add:

See Rev. Rul. 84-130, I.R.B. 1984-35, 5, holding that the employee's retained right to convert his group policy to a permanent individual policy upon his or her termination of employment is not an incident of ownership.

At the end of the third paragraph on page 225, add:

When a group life insurance policy has been assigned, the payments of premiums by the employer are treated as gifts made by the employee to the assignee. See Rev. Rul. 76-490, 1976-2 C.B. 300. The value of these gifts may be determined by the employee by using Table I under Reg. §1.79-3(d)(2). However, if the employee chooses not to use Table I for this purpose or if the plan is discriminatory and the employee is a *key* employee, the employee should use the actual cost allocable to the employee's insurance by obtaining the necessary information from the employer. Rev. Rul. 84-147, 1984-2 C.B. 201. If the group life insurance policy has been assigned to an irrevocable life insurance trust with little or no other assets where the beneficiaries have *Crummey* powers of withdrawal (see §10.47), the question arises as to how the withdrawal right may be satisfied. Letter Rul. 8021058 provides that the right may be satisfied by the assignment of the policy or an interest in the policy to the beneficiary.

In the sixth line from the top of page 226, the regulation citation is changed to read:

(See Reg. §§1.79-1(c)(2) and (3).)

At the end of the second sentence in the sixth paragraph on page 226, change the citation of the regulations to read:

See Reg. §§1.79-0 and 1.79-1(b).

At the end of the text on page 226 add:

The Tax Equity and Fiscal Responsibility Act of 1982 and the Deficit Reduction Act of 1984 made substantial revisions in the treatment of group life insurance. The $50,000 income tax exclusion for group term life insurance will be allowed to key employees only if the group plan is not discriminatory. I.R.C. §79(d). Generally, a discriminatory plan is one that favors key employees as to eligibility to participate or as to insurance benefits available.

A plan will not be discriminatory as to participants' eligibility if:

1. At least 70 per cent of all employees are covered.
2. At least 85 per cent of all participating employees are not "key" employees.
3. The Treasury Department finds the plan to be nondiscriminatory.
4. If the group life plan is provided under a cafeteria plan and the eligibility rules for cafeteria plans are met. See §13.7.

In meeting these tests, the following employees can be excluded:

1. Employees with less than three years of service.
2. Part-time and seasonal employees.
3. Certain nonresident aliens.
4. Employees covered by a collective bargaining agreement, if

group term life was the subject of good faith bargaining between the employer and employee representatives.

A *key* employee is generally (1) an officer with an annual compensation greater than $45,000 (under current law), (2) any one or more of the 10 employees with an annual compensation greater than $30,000 (under current law) who own (or are treated as owning under I.R.C. §318) the largest interest in the business, (3) an owner of more than five per cent of the business, or (4) an owner of more than one per cent of the business who receives more than $150,000 in compensation. See I.R.C. §§79(d)(b) and 416(i)(l) for elaboration and refinements on the general definition.

A plan will not be considered discriminatory as to insurance benefits if all benefits available to the key employees are also available to all the other participants, but the amount of insurance coverage provided can be based on the employee's compensation.

The new rules will inhibit the use of the permanent life insurance benefits and the retired lives reserve plans described in the text, because these plans typically have been designed to benefit only key employees. It may be too expensive for the employer to include these features in a group insurance plan that conforms to the new nondiscriminatory rules. Moreover, even if a retired lives reserve plan is nondiscriminatory, the cost of coverage over $50,000 of life insurance is included in the employee's taxable income. I.R.C. §79(e).

The Internal Revenue Service has issued a Technical Advice Memorandum regarding retired lives reserve plans which concludes that an employee, upon retirement, will receive taxable income by reason of the continuation of the group term life insurance, at least in those instances when the employee's interest in the fund becomes nonforfeitable. Letter Rul. 8342008.

The 1986 Tax Reform Act made significant changes to the taxation and nondiscrimination rules applicable to group term life insurance plans. See I.R.C. §89. The amendments will generally become effective after December 31, 1987. However, if the Treasury does not issue regulations under new I.R.C. §89 before October 1, 1987, these amendments will become effective three months after regulations are issued or December 31, 1988, whichever occurs first. See §1151(k)(1) of the Tax Reform Act of 1986. For special effective date rules for collective bargaining plans and certain group term insurance plans, see §1151(k)(2)-(5) of the Tax Reform Act of 1986.

Under I.R.C. §89(k), all employees will be taxed on the value of employer-provided group term life insurance, unless the coverage is stated in a formal group term life insurance plan document complying with the following provisions:

1.   The plan must be in writing;

2. The covered employees must have legally enforceable rights under the plan;
3. The employees are provided reasonable notification of benefits available to the plan;
4. The plan is maintained for the exclusive benefit of employees; and
5. The plan was established with the intention of being maintained for an indefinite period of time.

Under the nondiscrimination rules of I.R.C. §89(d), a plan will not be discriminatory as to participants' eligibility if:

1. At least 90 per cent of all employees who are not "highly compensated" employees are eligible to participate and have available a benefit that is at least 50 per cent of the largest employer-provided benefit available to any highly compensated employee;

2. At least 50 per cent of all employees eligible to participate in the plan are not "highly compensated" employees, or the ratio of highly compensated employees eligible to participate to the total number of highly compensated employees is no greater than the ratio of all eligible employees who are not highly compensated to the total number of employees who are not highly compensated; and

3. The plan does not implicitly or explicitly discriminate in favor of highly compensated employees.

In meeting these tests, the following employees are excluded from consideration: (1) employees with fewer than one year of service, or such shorter period specified by the plan; (2) employees who normally work less than 17-1/2 hours per week; (3) employees who normally work during not more than six months during any year; (4) employees under age 21; (5) certain nonresident aliens with no United States source income; and (6) employees covered by a collective bargaining agreement, if group term life insurance was the subject of good faith bargaining between the employer and employee representatives I.R.C. §89(h).

The 1986 Tax Reform Act also contains a benefit test with respect to certain statutory fringe benefits, including group term life insurance. Under I.R.C. §89(e), the average employer-provided benefit for employees other than highly compensated employees must be at least 75 per cent of the average employer-provided benefit for highly compensated employees under all plans of the employer of the same type. The "average employer-provided benefit" for each of the two specified groups of employees is determined by dividing all benefits provided to each respective group of employees by the number of members of that group, whether or not all members of the group are covered by the plans.

In applying the nondiscrimination tests of I.R.C. §89, the rules of I.R.C. §414(q) apply to determine who constitutes a "highly compensated employee." I.R.C. §89(j)(1). These are generally the uniform rules applied to qualified retirement plans. Thus, a highly compensated employee would be (1) an officer with an annual compensation greater than $45,000; (2) an employee who receives annual compensation in excess of $75,000; (3) any one or more of the top-paid 20 per cent of employees with an annual compensation greater than $50,000; or (4) an owner of more than 5 per cent of the business. See I.R.C. §§89(j)(1) and 414(q) for elaboration and refinements on the general definition.

I.R.C. §89(f) contains a special exception to the eligibility and benefit tests with respect to a group term life insurance plan. If at least 80 per cent of an employer's non-highly compensated employees are covered by the plan, and the plan does not by its terms or in practice discriminate with respect to eligibility in favor of highly compensated employees, then the plan will be treated as satisfying the eligibility and benefit tests of I.R.C. §89(d) and (e).

If the nondiscrimination rules of the Tax Reform Act of 1986 are violated during any plan year, the highly compensated employees who receive "excess benefits" under the plan during that year must include the amount of the excess benefits in gross income. See I.R.C. §89(b).

§10.57 B. Split-Dollar Life Insurance

At the end of the carryover paragraph on page 228, insert the following paragraph:

The Internal Revenue Service has, at least to some extent, changed its position regarding the estate taxability of split-dollar life insurance. It has now ruled that if the corporation, of which the decedent owned more than a 50 per cent interest, had the right to borrow against the cash surrender value of the policy, such right constitutes an incident of ownership by the decedent-insured in the entire policy. This incident of ownership causes the proceeds to be taxable in the decedent's estate. Rev. Rul. 82-145, I.R.B. 1982-31, 7. It is not certain what the Internal Revenue Service's position would be if the corporation had no right to borrow against the policy's cash surrender value, but merely had a collateral assignment securing the repayment of the loan in the event of the decedent's death. Arguably, the collateral assignment is not an incident of ownership in the policy.

At the end of the text on page 228, add the following:

For the possible alternative minimum tax consequences of a corporation owning a life insurance policy, see Supplement §12.14.

§10.59   A. Universal Life Insurance (New)

One of the advantages of life insurance, as an estate planning tool, is that it receives favorable income tax treatment. The proceeds payable by reason of the death of the insured are generally not subject to income tax. I.R.C. §101(a). See §10.21. Another favorable income tax characteristic of life insurance is that the "interest" credited to the cash value of the policy is not then subject to income tax as far as the policy holder is concerned. (See, however, §10.30 for a discussion of possible income tax liability if the policy is surrendered prior to the insured's death).

In order to take greater advantage of these income tax characteristics, a new product has recently been developed by the life insurance industry, called "universal" or "flexible premium" life insurance. These policies have several characteristics not present in a typical ordinary life insurance policy. First, a competitive rate of interest, sometimes tied to the treasury bill rate or other money market index but with a guaranteed minimum rate of usually 4 per cent, will be credited to the policy. Second, the policy holder can change, within broad limits, the amount and frequency of the premiums which are to be paid under the policy. Normally, the greater the interest rate and the amount of premiums paid, the greater the death benefit will be. Theoretically, however, the policy could be structured so that the holder could invest a substantial cash amount, without increasing the insurance death benefit, but greatly increasing the cash value in the policy. This buildup in the cash value could be used to reduce future premiums on a given amount of life insurance or provide a larger amount to the holder if surrendered before death for its cash value. In any event, the interest earned on the cash value will not be subject to current income tax.

Without corrective legislation, it is clear that a universal life insurance policy, as well as other policies where the death benefit does not increase with the amount of premiums paid, could be used as a tax-free or tax-deferred savings plan. However, the Deficit Reduction Act of 1984 provides guidelines with which a policy must comply in order to be treated as life insurance for income tax purposes. To exclude from gross income the entire death benefit proceeds of a life insurance policy as well as the "interest" earned on the cash value, one of two requirements must be satisfied during the entire time that the policy is held. I.R.C. §7702.

Under the first requirement, two tests must be met. I.R.C.

§§7702(a)(2), (c) and (d). First, under a premium test, in general, the sum of the premiums paid cannot exceed the greater of (1) the single premium necessary to fund the contract at the time of the issuance of the policy, or (2) the sum of the level premiums necessary (based on specified assumptions) to fund future benefits under the contract. Second, under a *cash value corridor* requirement, at any given age the policy death benefit must exceed the policy cash value by a particular percentage. These percentages start at 250 for age 40 and reduce gradually until age 75. For ages 75 through 90 the percentage remains at 105, and at age 91 the percentage decreases 1 per cent each year until 100 per cent is reached at age 95.

The second alternative requirement is met if the cash value does not at any time exceed the net single premium necessary (based on specified assumptions) to fund future contract benefits. I.R.C. §§7702(a)(1) and (b).

XI. Recommended Reading

Insert after Munch in the recommended reading list on page 230:

Saks, "Survivor Joint Life Policies Will Flourish As A Result Of The Economic Recovery Tax" 9 *Estate Planning* 117 (1982).

Insert after Wark in the recommended reading list on page 230:

Weinstock, "Irrevocable Trust for Life Insurance More Effective Than Marital Deduction" 10 *Estate Planning* 258 (1983).

"Insurance Developments Since ERTA" 17 *Real Prop, Prob and Tr J* 527 (1982).

Annuities

11

II. Commercial Annuities

C. Taxation

§11.8   1. Income Tax

The last two sentences of the last paragraph on page 234 are deleted and the following is inserted:

The Tax Reform Act of 1986 modified the use of the exclusion ratio. With respect to annuities with a starting date after 1986, the total amounts excluded (i.e., the nontaxable parts) may not exceed the unrecovered investment in the contract. Accordingly, in the above example, if A outlives his 15-year life expectancy, no part of the $500 per month payment will thereafter be excludable from gross income. I.R.C. §72(b)(2). Conversely, if he dies before he has recovered his investment in the contract (i.e., prior to the end of 15 years), the unrecovered investment will be deductible in his last income tax return. I.R.C. §72(b)(3).

The Treasury Department, with respect to investments in annuity contracts made after June 30, 1986, has changed the annuity tables which must be used in computing the expected return. The new regulations make the life expectancy multiples gender neutral and also, based on recent experience, increase the life expectance probabilities over what they were in old tables. Reg. §1.72-9. See Table IX.A in Appendix to Supplement. In the above example, A, under the new table, would have a life expectancy of 20 years (rather than 15); the expected return would be $120,000, and the exclusion ratio would be 58.333 per cent ($70,000 - $120,000) rather than 77.777 per cent.

For a discussion of the income tax consequences of a gift of an annuity contract, see §11.9 of the Supplement.

The Tax Equity and Fiscal Responsibility Act of 1982 added a 5 per cent penalty tax for early withdrawals from an annuity contract, and the Tax Reform Act of 1986 increased the penalty to 10 per cent. For a full discussion, see Supplement §11.11.

The Deficit Reduction Act of 1984 provides that an annuity contract must include specific rules for distribution in the event of the owner's death. The contract must provide that:

1. If the owner dies on or after the annuity starting date, any remaining undistributed portion of the annuity will be distributed at least as rapidly as under the method of distribution in effect at the owner's death, and

2. If the owner dies before the annuity starting date, the entire interest in the annuity contract must be distributed within five years of the date of death.

However, the annuity may provide that distributions will be payable over the lifetime of the beneficiaries if such distributions are scheduled to begin within one year of the owner's death. Moreover, if the beneficiary is a spouse of the owner, the annuity may be continued in the name of the spouse as the new owner. I.R.C. §72(s).

If a contract issued after January 18, 1985, does not include these provisions, it will not be taxed as an annuity and hence the payment will generally be treated as income. See Reg. §1.72-1(d).

The Tax Reform Act of 1986 modified the above distribution requirements by providing that, if there are joint owners of the contract, the mandated distribution will be triggered on the death of the first of them to die. It also provides that the distribution requirements do not apply to qualified retirement plans or individual retirement annuities. I.R.C. §72(s).

§11.9 2. Gift Tax

At the end of the text on page 235 add:

See also proposed Reg. §25.2523(f)-1(c)(2).

The Tax Reform Act of 1986 treats the gift of an annuity contract issued after April 22, 1987, as an assignment for income tax purposes. It requires the annuity holder to report in income the amount by which the net surrender value of the contract exceeds the investment in the contract. I.R.C. §72(e)(4)(C). For the definition of "investment in the contract" see §11.8. The donee will receive a new basis in the contract equal to the donor's investment in the contract, plus the amount includable in the donor's income. I.R.C. §72(e)(4)(C)(iii). These rules do not apply if the gift is made to the donor's spouse or, if made in connection with a divorce, to a former spouse. I.R.C. §72(e)(4)(C)(ii).

§11.11   D. Tax Deferred Variable and Investment Annuities

The last sentence of the fourth paragraph on page 236 is changed to read:

Often, the income earned on the assets in the latter type of annuity is currently taxable to the owner. *Christofferson v US* 84-2 USTC ¶9990 (1984); see Rev. Rul. 82-55, 82-1 C.B. 12; Rev. Rul. 81-225, 1981-2 C.B. 12; Rev. Rul. 80-274, 1980-2 C.B. 27; Rev. Rul. 77-85, 1977-1 C.B. 12.

At the end of the text on page 236 add:

The Tax Equity and Fiscal Responsibility Act of 1982, the Deficit Reduction Act of 1984, and the Tax Reform Act of 1986 significantly changed the income taxability of withdrawals from tax deferred annuities, whether of the variable or investment type. Amounts received before the starting date of the annuity will now be treated first as withdrawals of income to the extent of the income earned on the investment in the contract. I.R.C. §72(e)(2)(B)(i). Only withdrawals in excess of the amount of such income will be treated as a return of capital.

If the policy holder borrows against the annuity contract or assigns or pledges the contract, any amounts received will be treated as amounts withdrawn from the contract and be taxed to the extent of the unwithdrawn income earned on the investment in the contract, i.e., on a first in/first out basis. I.R.C. §72(e)(4)(A). If the loan is repaid, it will be treated as an additional investment in the contract.

The new rules generally apply to withdrawals made after August 13, 1982. For contracts in existence prior to August 14, 1982, the old rules will apply, unless additional investments are made in the contract. In that case, the portion of the income earned on the later investments will be treated under the new rules.

To further discourage the use of deferred annuities as short-term investments, early withdrawals made prior to the annuity starting date, will be subject to an additional 10 per cent penalty tax. I.R.C. §72(q). The penalty generally applies to all amounts which are included in income.

The 10 per cent penalty tax will not apply to certain distributions which in the main are (1) made on or after the date the policy holder attains age 59 1/2; (2) made to a death beneficiary under the contract; (3) attributable to the policy holder's becoming disabled; (4) one of a series of substantially equal periodic payments made for the life of the taxpayer or the joint lives of the taxpayer and the beneficiary; or (5) from a qualified retirement plan (see §13.9). I.R.C. §72(q)(2).

It appears that when the owner of the annuity contract dies, even before the starting date, the contract will not receive a stepped-up basis, but the payments received will be taxed as an annuity. See I.R.C. §1014(b)(9)(A). For a discussion of how annuity is taxed, see §11.8.

III. Private Annuities

A. Taxation

§11.13   1. Death Taxation

Add at the end of the text on page 237:

But see *LaFargue v Commr* 689 F2d 845 (9th Cir 1982). This is an income tax case which holds that a private annuity sale may be made to a trust and taxed as such, provided the annuity was not calculated to approximate the annual income from the property and the seller did not continue to control the property after the sale. See also *Stern v Commr* 747 F2d 555 (9th Cir 1984) (84-2 USTC ¶9949). The Tax Court in a later opinion held that if the above criteria are met, the transferred property will not be included in the seller's estate. *Estate of Fabric* 83 TC 932 (1984). But see Letter Rul. 8223014 where the seller was treated as having retained an income interest in a trust, rather than a life annuity, because the payments to be made to the seller were not calculated to return all of the principal to him during his lifetime.

§11.14   2. Gift Taxes

At the end of the text on page 237 add:

Because of new valuation tables (see Appendix VIII of the Supplement for explanation), new calculations should be substituted in the example in the text. In the example, the annuity factor at age 65 is now 6.7970 (see Supplement Appendix VIII, Table A). To avoid gift tax liability, the yearly annuity payments, therefore, should now be $14,712 ($100,000 divided by 6.7970). If they are less, the difference, when multiplied by 6.7970, will be the amount of the gift.

3. Income Taxes

§11.15   a. Of the Transferor—Annuitant

Following the example on page 238, add the following new paragraph:

Because of the new life expectancy table in Reg. §1.72-9 (see Appendix IX.A.), new calculations should be substituted in the example in the text if the annuity transaction was entered into after June 30, 1986.

§11.16   b. Of the Transferee—Payor

Before the last paragraph on page 239, add the following new paragraph:

Because of the new life expectancy table in Reg. §1.72-9 (see Appendix IX.A.), new calculations should be substituted in the example in the text if the annuity transaction was entered into after June 30, 1986.

Handling a Business Interest 12

II. Valuation of a Closely Held Business Interest for Death Tax Purposes

§12.6 D. Interest of Owner

The official citation of Estate of Bright v US in the second sentence of the third paragraph on page 250 is now:

658 F2d 999·(5th Cir 1981).

At the end of the last sentence of the text on page 250 add:

See also *Estate of Propstra v US* 680 F2d 1248 (9th Cir 1982) (82-2 USTC ¶13,475), where the court held that the value of a decedent's one-half undivided interest in a community property asset could receive a discount even if the husband and wife together owned a 100 per cent interest in the asset. The Tax Court applied the holding in *Estate of Bright* for gift tax purposes and permitted a minority interest discount in valuing the gift of shares of stock in a family owned corporation. *Ward v Commr* 87 TC 78 (1986).

III.　Buy-Sell Agreements

§12.9　C. Making the Price Binding for Tax Purposes

At the end of the first sentence of the last paragraph on page 251 add:

See also *St. Louis County Bank v US* 674 F2d 1207 (8th Cir 1982).

E.　Paying the Purchase Price

§12.14　1. Through Life Insurance

The following paragraph is added at the end of the text on page 253:

The Tax Reform Act of 1986 introduced a possible disadvantage in having the corporation own life insurance, because the annual increase in the policy's value as well as the receipt of the life insurance proceeds may cause the corporation to be subject to the alternative minimum tax. The alternative minimum taxable income of a corporation for tax years beginning in 1987, 1988, and 1989 must include one-half of the amount by which the corporation's adjusted net book income exceeds its alternative minimum taxable income (computed without regard to this excess). I.R.C. §56(f). While the annual increase in the value of the policy and the receipt of the proceeds of life insurance are exempt from taxable income (I.R.C. §101(a)), each of these items will increase the corporation's book income.

G.　Form of Agreement

§12.24　1. Partnership Buy-Sell Agreement

At the end of the text on page 257 add:

Absent a buy-sell agreement, the death of a partner does not close the partnership year. I.R.C. §706(c). Accordingly, when a partner dies, his or her share of the partnership income or loss for the partnership year that ends after the partner's death will be includable in the estate's income tax return, rather than in the decedent's final income tax return. This result may be advantageous or disadvantageous depending on whether a lower or higher income tax will result from reporting the deceased's partner's share on the estate income tax return, rather than on the decedent's final return. However, when there is a buy-sell agreement, the partnership year with respect to the deceased partner's interest will close as of the date of sale. If the sale under the buy-sell agreement occurs as of the date of death, then the year is deemed to close on the date of death and the deceased partner's share of the partnership income or loss will be includable in the decedent's final return. Reg. §1.706-1(c)(3)(iv).

2. Corporate Buy-Sell Agreement

a. Where Stock Redemption Is Preferable

§12.26   i. More Economical

The following is added at the end of the text on page 258:

For the possible alternative minimum tax consequences of a corporation owning a life insurance policy, see Supplement §12.14.

§12.29   iv. Appreciated Assets

Delete the citation at the end of the second sentence of the second paragraph on page 259 and insert:

See Bittker and Eustice, *Federal Income Taxation of Corporations and Shareholders* ¶9.63 (Warren, Gorham and Lamont Inc 4th ed 1979).

At the end of the text on page 259 add:

The Tax Equity and Fiscal Responsibility Act of 1982 amended I.R.C. §311(d)(2)(A) by changing the requirements which must be satisfied so that a corporation can avoid taxable gain on the distribution of appreciated assets. I.R.C. §311(d)(2). Taxable gain can no longer be avoided where an estate owns at least 10 per cent of the outstanding stock of the corporation for at least 12 months prior to such distribution. However, a corporation can continue to avoid taxable gain if the distribution of appreciated assets meets the requirements of I.R.C. §303. See §§12.36 and 12.38.

A new exception permitting the avoidance of gain was enacted, namely, where the distribution, among other requirements, is to a shareholder, who owns "qualified" stock. "Qualified" stock is stock that was held by a 10 per cent or more noncorporate shareholder for at least five years or since the date of inception of the corporation, whichever is less. I.R.C. §311(e). This exception may not be of much use to a shareholder's estate, because it is unlikely that the estate will have owned the stock for five years. As a result, the principal method for a corporation to avoid taxable gain on the distribution of appreciated assets will now be by use of an I.R.C. §303 redemption.

The Tax Reform Act of 1986 eliminated all relevant exceptions, including the exception for an I.R.C. §303 redemption, to the general rule that a corporation will recognize taxable gain on the distribution of appreciated assets. See §631(c) of the Tax Reform Act of 1986. Accordingly, the use of appreciated assets to purchase the decedent's stock is no longer a viable tax tool.

b.   Where Cross-Purchase Agreement Is Preferable

§12.33   iii. Tax Consequences

The fourth and fifth paragraphs on page 261 are changed to read:

While one would expect the payment by the corporation to the estate in redemption of the stock to be treated as a capital transaction, this is not always the case. The general rule is that any distribution by a corporation to a shareholder with respect to its stock, to the extent of the corporation's earnings and profits, will be taxed as a dividend, unless a specific exception applies. I.R.C. §301. I.R.C. §302, as amended by the Tax Equity and Fiscal Responsibility Act of 1982, lists four exceptions. The redemption payment will not be considered a dividend if it completely terminates the stockholder's interest in the corporation (§302(b)(3)), if it is substantially disproportionate (§302(b)(2)), if it is a partial liquidation (§302(b)(4)), or if it is not essentially equivalent to a dividend (§302(b)(1)). If, however, none of these four exceptions applies, the proceeds of the redemption will, to the extent that the corporation has earnings and profits, be taxable as a dividend to the deceased shareholder's estate rather than as a capital transaction.

In order for the redemption to completely terminate a shareholder's interest, all of his or her stock must be redeemed by the corporation. In order to have a substantially disproportionate redemption, the shareholder, immediately after the redemption must own less than 50 per cent of the corporation's voting stock, and the percentage of voting stock which he or she owns in the corporation after the redemption must be at least 20 per cent less than the percentage was prior to the redemption. In order to have a partial liquidation, among other requirements, the corporation must contract its business, which is an element not present in the typical buy-sell situation. The most common way to avoid dividend taxation as a result of the death of a shareholder is to have the redemption qualify as a complete or substantially disproportionate redemption.

The second sentence (including the citations) of the first full paragraph on page 262 is changed to read:

The attribution rules of §318 must be applied in determining whether the redemption is not essentially equivalent to a dividend. *US v Davis* 397 US 30 (1970).

At the end of item 3 c. on page 263 add:

The Tax Equity and Fiscal Responsibility Act of 1982 amended the code to specifically permit an estate or trust to waive the family attribution rules. However, the family members through whom stock ownership is attributed to the estate or trust must join in making the waiver, and both the family members and the estate or trust must meet the requirements stated in items a., b. and c. above. I.R.C. §302(c)(2)(C). Thus, if all the stock of a corporation is owned by a father and a son, the father dies and the mother is the sole beneficiary of the father's estate, the mother and the estate may waive the attribution of the son's stock to the mother and thereby to the estate. As a result, the redemption of all of the estate's stock would qualify as a dividend-free complete termination of the estate's interest.

IV.   Use of §303 Redemption

§12.35   A. The Problem

The first sentence of the second paragraph on page 264 is changed to read as follows:

Providing certain requirements are met, §303 of the Internal Revenue Code permits the redemption of that portion of the stock of a deceased shareholder which does not exceed in value the sum of the federal and state death taxes, including the generation-skipping transfer tax, and funeral and administration expenses without having the proceeds taxed to his estate as a dividend.

§12.38   D. Using §303 Even if Liquidity is Not Needed

At the end of the first paragraph on page 266 add:

The §303 redemption proceeds, to the extent that the redemption price exceeds the amount properly chargeable to the capital account, will reduce the earnings and profits account of the corporation for the purpose of determining the extent to which future distributions will be taxed as a dividend. I.R.C. §316; Rev. Rul. 79-376, 1979-2 CB 133. This reduction will also lessen the possibility of a future unreasonable accumulation of surplus problem. See §12.37.

At the end of the text on page 267, add:

The Tax Reform Act of 1986 eliminated the corporation's ability to use appreciated assets to redeem stock under I.R.C. §303 without the corporation's realizing any gain on the distribution. See §631(c) of the Tax Reform Act of 1986.

V.   Recapitalizing Stock of Closely Held Company

§12.41   C. Typical Plan of Recapitalization

Item 1 in the second paragraph on page 268 is changed to read:

1.   Each share will have a par value of $100 per share, and a redemption price of $77 per share.

Item 4 in the second paragraph on page 268 is changed to read:

4.   In the event of the liquidation of the company for any reason each share will receive $77 per share, before anything is paid to the common stock.

The last paragraph on page 268 is changed to read:

One of the reasons for assigning the above characteristics to each class of stock is to attempt to peg the value of each class for tax purposes. The Internal Revenue Service has promulgated guidelines to be considered in valuing preferred and common stock of a closely held corporation in a recapitalization. The factors to be used in valuing the preferred stock include its yield, dividend coverage, protection of its liquidation preference, its redemption privilege and voting rights. Rev. Rul. 83-120, I.R.B. 1983-33, 8. Where the common stock has the exclusive right to the benefits of future appreciation of the value of the corporation, the common stock will, in the view of the Service, have substantial value and it will not be possible to assign all of the present value of the corporation to the preferred stock. An expert business appraiser should be retained to value the company and each class of stock before the recapitalization is consummated. Assume the preferred stock has a value of $700,000 at the time of issuance and the total value of both classes of common stock is $300,000. As the company prospers and increases in value, the preferred stock in all likelihood will not be worth more than $770,000, its liquidation value, and the entire excess will be represented by the value of the common stock. As between the voting and nonvoting common, the Internal Revenue Service may argue that the voting common should be valued at a premium because only this stock has the vote, which is a valuable right. See *Estate of Lee v Commr* 69 TC 860 (1978) nonacq 1980-1 CB 2.

Delete the third sentence of the first paragraph on the top of page 269 and insert:

At most, the nonvoting common will be worth $297,000 ($300,000 times 990/1,000) for gift tax purposes. Unless the donor's remaining gift tax equivalent exemption (see Appendix IV) is less than $297,000, there will be no gift tax actually payable.

The second paragraph on page 269 is changed to read:

Substantial estate taxes will be saved, by reason of the above plan. Using another example, assume on the estate owner's death, the company is worth $2,000,000. It is likely that the preferred stock will have a value of approximately $770,000. The remaining $1,230,000 of value will be assigned to the common stock. If each share of voting and nonvoting common is held to be of equal value, the voting common will be worth $12,300 ($1,230,000 times 10/1000), and the nonvoting common, $1,217,700 ($1,230,000 times 990/1000). Even assuming that each share of voting common stock, because it has voting rights, is worth twice as much as each share of nonvoting common stock, the voting common will be worth $24,600, and the nonvoting common, $1,205,400. Based on the latter assumption, the total value of the preferred and voting common stock included in the estate owner's estate will be $794,600. Assuming further that no part of the $297,000 gift of the nonvoting common stock qualified for the gift tax annual exclusion, the entire amount of the gift will be added to the taxable estate, resulting in the total value of $1,091,600. If the estate owner had not recapitalized the stock and had not gifted the nonvoting common, a total value of $2,000,000 would have been included.

At the end of the last paragraph of the text on page 269 add:

But see Rev. Proc. 82-28, 1982-1 C.B. 480, where the Internal Revenue Service states that it will not issue income tax rulings on partnership freezes involving family partnerships. Apparently the matter is under study and a definitive revenue ruling will be published setting forth the views of the Internal Revenue Service on the income tax consequences of family partnership freezes.

D. Special Tax Problems Incident to Reorganization

§12.42   1. Income Tax

At the end of the first paragraph on page 270 insert:

When the preferred stock has an unreasonable redemption premium, it will be treated as a distribution on preferred stock giving rise to a dividend under I.R.C. §§305(b)(4) and 305(c). A redemption premium not in excess of 10 per cent of the issue price will, however, be considered a reasonable premium. Reg. §1.305(b)(2). The issue price for purposes of determining the 10 per cent "safe harbor" requirement is not the par or stated value of the preferred stock, but the actual value at the time of issuance. Rev. Rul. 83-119, I.R.B. 1983-33, 6.

§12.43   2. Gift Tax

The first three sentences are changed to read:

As indicated in §12.41, it is unlikely that a gift of the nonvoting common stock, issued in the typical plan of recapitalization, will give rise to an actual gift tax because of the availability of the equivalent exemption. If the characteristics of the preferred stock are not carefully planned, however, the value of the gifted stock may exceed the estate owner's unused equivalent exemption. In that event, the gift of the nonvoting common stock may give rise to gift tax.

§12.44   3. Estate Tax

After the third sentence on page 271, add:

See also Letter Rul. 8504011 where the gifted common stock was included in the donor's estate because the retained preferred stock was entitled, under a rather unusual plan of recapitalization, to participate in almost all of the dividends that would ever be paid by the corporation.

VI. Use of Deferred Compensation Contracts

C. Tax Considerations

§12.47 1. Death Tax

At the end of the second paragraph on page 272, add the following:

See also *Estate of Glen J Van Wye v Commr* 686 F2d 425 (6th Cir 1982) (82-2 USTC ¶13,485).

The last two sentences of the last paragraph on page 272 are changed to read:

It should be remembered that if the beneficiary is a living trust that the employee during his or her lifetime has the right to revoke or amend, he or she thereby will indirectly have the right to change the beneficiary, even if the contract specifically excludes such right. If one wishes to utilize a revocable living trust (see Chapter 7) in a given estate plan and name this trust as the death beneficiary under the deferred compensation contract, the trust itself should provide that the employee's right to revoke or amend the trust does not extend to any death proceeds payable under such deferred compensation contract.

In a favorable private letter ruling, the Internal Revenue Service held that a death benefit payable to an employee's irrevocable beneficiary was not includable in the employee's estate, even though the "death benefit only" contract was between the employee and a corporation in which the employee was a majority shareholder. Letter Rul. 8701003.

§12.48 2. Gift Tax

This section is changed to read:

In its continuing efforts to prevent "death benefit only" contracts from escaping taxation, the Internal Revenue Service contends that the employee who does not retain any rights or benefits in the contract during his or her lifetime (see §12.47) has made a completed gift of the contractual benefits to the irrevocable beneficiary at the time the employee dies. Rev. Rul. 81-31, 1981-1 C.B. 475. The Tax Court disagreed with the Internal Revenue Service's theory and held that a "death benefit only" contract of the type described above does not result in a taxable gift by the employee. *Estate of DiMarco* 87 TC 653 (1986).

VII.   Election to Defer Payment of Estate Tax with Respect to Closely Held Business Interest

§12.51   A. Introduction

The first sentence on page 273 is changed to read as follows:

Where an interest in a closely held business or farm constitutes more than a designated percentage of the estate and certain other requirements are met, the executor may elect to pay a portion of the estate tax and generation-skipping transfer tax resulting from direct skips in deferred installments.

B.   Decedents Dying After 1981

§12.52   1. In General

The first sentence beginning on page 273 is changed to read as follows:

If the requirements described in §§12.53 and 12.54 are met, the payment of that portion of the estate tax and generation-skipping transfer tax resulting from direct skips attributable to the estate owner's interest in a closely held business or farm may be made over a 15-year period.

At the end of the text on page 274 add:

The Tax Equity and Fiscal Responsibility Act of 1982 sets forth a new procedure for determining the rate of interest on tax deficiencies and deferred tax payments (except for the portion qualifying for the 4 per cent rate). The interest rate will be adjusted each September 30 and March 31, based on the previous six-month adjusted prime rate. The new adjusted rate will be effective for the six-month period that starts the following January 1 and July 1, respectively. I.R.C. §6621(b). Rev. Rul. 85-169, I.R.B. 1985-44. All interest will be compounded daily. I.R.C. §6622.

The Tax Reform Act of 1986 generally disallows an interest deduction for interest paid by a noncorporate taxpayer on a tax deficiency. However, there is a special exception allowing the deduction for interest paid on an I.R.C. §6166 deferral. See I.R.C. §163(h)(2)(E).

2. Requirements

§12.53   a. Percentage Requirements

At the end of the second sentence of the first paragraph on page 274 add:

The gross estate is reduced by all expenses and losses even though the estate elects (see §15.15) to claim some or all of these items as deductions on its income tax return rather than on the federal estate tax return. Letter Rul. 8203009.

At the end of the first paragraph on page 274 add:

The Technical Corrections Act of 1982 provides that an estate shall be treated as meeting the 35 per cent requirement only if the estate meets the test both with and without including gifts made within three years of death. I.R.C. §2035(d)(4). See T.A.M. 8527003.

§12.54   b. Must Constitute a "Closely" Held Business

At the end of the last paragraph on page 275, delete Letter Rul. 8136022 and insert:

Letter Rul. 8240055.

Under an amendment made to I.R.C. §6166 by the Deficit Reduction Act of 1984, the value of an interest in a closely-held business entity will no longer include the value of that entity's passive assets, that is, assets not used in carrying on a trade or business. I.R.C. §6166(b)(9). The Act also permits an estate to treat stock in certain holding companies that own stock in a company actively engaged in a trade or business as stock in the active company. Even if a holding company qualifies as a trade or business, the special 4 per cent interest rate will not be permitted and only a 10-year, rather than a 15-year, period of deferral will be allowed. I.R.C. §6166(b)(8).

§12.57   D. Pitfalls in Planning to Use Election

Item 2 on page 276 is changed to read:

2.   Except for the 4 per cent interest rate payable on that portion of the estate tax attributable to the first $1,000,000 in value of a closely held business, the rate of interest is adjustable semiannually by the Treasury Department in accordance with changes in the adjusted prime rate, and compounds daily, I.R.C. §6621(b). Although this interest rate is currently 11 per cent (see Supplement §12.52), the rate or rates in effect during the period or periods when the tax remained unpaid control, rather than the one in effect at the time the obligation arises. Since the rate of interest is subject to change every six months, for planning purposes it is impossible to know the eventual interest cost.

VIII.   Considering Disposition of Business Interest before Death

§12.59   B. Outright Sale for Cash

At the end of the text on page 278, add:

The Tax Reform Act of 1986 changed the capital gains tax rate. See Supplement §2.52 for an explanation.

X.   Recommended Reading

Insert after Abbin in the recommended reading list on page 283:

Adams, Sweet and Beiber, "Recapitalizations Revisited" 123 No 8 *Trusts and Estates* 21 (1984).

Insert after Herwitz in the recommended reading list on page 283:

Kahn, "Closely Held Stocks: Deferral and Financing of Estate Tax Costs Through Sections 303 and 6166" 35 *The Tax Lawyer* 639 (1982).

Insert after Kanter in the recommended reading list on page 283:

Kaplan, "Freezing Estate Tax Value of Closely Held Businesses" 19 *Real Prop, Prob and Tr J* 32 (1984).

Insert after Osach in the recommended reading list on page 284:

Owen, "Attribution Rule Changes of TEFRA" 58 *Journal of Taxation* 202 (1983).

Employee Benefits

13

I. Introduction

§13.3 C. Requirement of Employment Relationship

At the end of the first paragraph on page 287 insert:

The Tax Equity and Fiscal Responsibility Act of 1982 removes most of the advantages of a corporate retirement plan compared to a self-employed retirement plan, commencing in 1984. See §13.19.

The citation at the end of the first sentence of the last paragraph on page 287 is changed to read:

See I.R.C. §§1361 to 1379

At the end of the last paragraph of the text on page 287 add:

The Tax Equity and Fiscal Responsibility Act of 1982 removes, for the most part, the disparity between benefits and contributions to self-employment retirement plans and corporate plans, commencing in 1984. See §13.19. As a result, a greater than 5 per cent shareholder of a Subchapter S corporation will no longer be treated differently than an employee—shareholder of a regular corporation.

II. Medical Reimbursement Plans

§13.4 A. Income Tax Consequences

At the end of the text on page 288, add:

Many technical requirements have been introduced by the Tax Reform Act of 1986 to prevent employers from providing certain fringe benefits, including medical reimbursement plans, which discriminate in favor of highly compensated employees. These requirements, which will apply to both insured and noninsured medical reimbursement plans, are generally not effective until after 1988. It is anticipated that detailed regulations will be issued prior to that time. Hence, these requirements are not discussed in this Supplement.

§13.5 B. Application to Owner-Employee of Closely Held Corporation

At the end of the text on page 288, add:

For the effect of the 1986 Tax Reform Act, see Supplement §13.4.

§13.6 III. Group Legal Services Plan

The second sentence of the first paragraph on page 289 is changed to read:

It is effective for a trial period ending before 1988.

§13.7 IV. Cafeteria Plans

At the end of the text on page 290, add:

For the effect of the Tax Reform Act on the nondiscrimination rules relating to cafeteria plans, see Supplement §13.4.

V.   Qualified Retirement Plans

A.   Corporate Plans

§13.9   1. Requirements for Qualification

At the end of the first paragraph on page 291 insert:

For tax years beginning after 1983, stricter qualification requirements have been imposed on top-heavy plans, see §13.13A of this
Supplement for a full discussion.

Many technical changes have been introduced by the Tax Reform
Act of 1986 relating to the requirements for qualification of retirement
plans. In general, these revised requirements are not effective until
plan years beginning in 1989. It is anticipated that detailed regulations
will be issued prior to that date. Hence, these requirements are not
discussed in this Supplement.

§13.13A a. What Are Top-Heavy Plans? (New)

The Tax Equity and Fiscal Responsibility Act of 1982 imposed
stricter qualification requirements on so-called "top-heavy" plans. In
general, a top-heavy-defined contribution plan is one in which more
than 60 per cent of the total account balances are provided for "key"
employees. A defined benefit plan is considered top-heavy if more than
60 per cent of the total present value of the accumulated accrued
benefits are for "key" employees. I.R.C. §416(g). Key employees are
generally defined as officers, any one or more of the 10 employees
owning the largest interest in the business, 5 per cent owners, or 1 per
cent owners who have annual compensation of more than $150,000.
Most closely held corporations will be subject to the top-heavy rules,
if only because their plans must include provisions that would
automatically take effect in the event the plan becomes top-heavy in
the future. I.R.C. §401(a)(10)(B)(ii).

In order to have a top-heavy plan qualify for the favorable tax
treatment accorded an exempt retirement plan, several special requirements must be met.

First, more rapid vesting is required (see §13.9). There must either
be full vesting of the employee's benefits within three years, or graded
vesting with steps of 20 per cent after the second year and full (100
per cent) vesting at the end of the sixth year.

Second, top-heavy plans must provide certain minimum benefits or
contributions to nonkey employees. If the plan is a defined benefit
plan, the minimum pension for each nonkey employee must generally

be 2 per cent of the employee's average compensation earned during the five highest salary years, multiplied by the number of years of service, but not to exceed 20 per cent of his or her average compensation earned during the highest five salary years. I.R.C. §416(c)(1). In a defined contribution plan, the employer generally must contribute a minimum of 3 per cent of the employee's compensation for that year. I.R.C. §416(c)(2).

Third, in all top-heavy plans, the maximum yearly compensation that generally may be used to determine the employee's benefits from or contributions to the plan may not exceed $200,000. Such amount will, however, starting in 1986, be adjusted by changes in the cost of living index. I.R.C. §416(d). The effect of this required ceiling is to reduce the value of the retirement plan for persons earning over the ceiling amount. When such highly paid person is an owner of the business and whose objective in having a retirement plan is primarily for personal benefit, the effective cost for providing such benefit will increase.

For the effect of the Tax Reform Act of 1986 regarding the requirements for qualification of a retirement plan, see Supplement §13.9.

5.   Tax Aspects of Qualified Plans

§13.14   a. Employer's Contributions

At the end of the second paragraph on page 294 add:

The Tax Equity and Fiscal Responsibility Act of 1982 changed the limits on benefits and contributions. The previous limits have, in general, been reduced from $136,425 and $45,475 to $90,000 and $30,000 respectively, with limited cost of living adjustments. I.R.C. §§415(b), (c) and (d).

The Tax Reform Act of 1986 requires for all plans, regardless of whether or not they are top-heavy, a $200,000 maximum yearly compensation limit that may be used to determine the employee's benefits from or contributions to the plan. I.R.C.§§401(a)(7) and 404(1).

c. Taxability of Employee Benefits

§13.16   i. Income Tax

At the end of the first sentence of the third paragraph on page 295, insert the following:

In order to prevent tax deferral for too long a period, the Tax Equity and Fiscal Responsibility Act of 1982 requires that retirement distributions under all qualified plans must begin at actual retirement or age 70 1/2, whichever is later. However, where the plan is top-heavy (see §13.13A of this Supplement), and commencing in 1989 for all plans (see I.R.C. §401(a)(9)(C)), the distributions must begin at age 70 1/2 regardless of the actual retirement age. Also, with certain exemptions such as an annuity payable to the employee's spouse, death benefits, where retirement distributions have not begun prior to the employee's death, must be completely distributed within five years of the employee's death. I.R.C. §401(a)(9). However, the five-year rule generally does not apply if the death benefit is payable to a designated beneficiary; the amount payable will be distributed over the beneficiary's life (or life expectancy) and the distribution begins no later than one year after the employee's death. I.R.C. §401(a)(9)(B)(iii). Moreover, the Tax Reform Act of 1986 imposes, starting in 1989, a 50 per cent excise tax on the person receiving the distribution, to the extent the amount received is less than the required minimum amount. I.R.C. §4974(a). There is, however, an exemption for benefits payable to an employee who made a beneficiary designation prior to January 1, 1984, under the Tax Equity and Fiscal Responsibility Act of 1982. Act §1121(d)(4) of the Tax Reform Act of 1986. *By reason of the repeal of the three-year basis recovery rule by §1122(h)(2) of the Tax Reform Act of 1986, the last sentence of the fourth paragraph on page 295 is deleted.*

The second and third sentences of the fifth paragraph on page 295 are changed to read:

First of all, if the lump sum payment or, under certain circumstances, at least 50 per cent of the distributable amount, is transferred or *rolled over* within 60 days into an individual retirement account (see §13.20) or to a new employer's qualified plan, the distribution is not taxed. I.R.C. §402(a)(5). The surviving spouse of an employee may also roll over a lump sum distribution, or 50 per cent of the distribution, into an individual retirement account.

At the end of the carryover paragraph on page 296, insert:

The capital gains treatment for distributions attributable to pre-1974 contributions is phased out over a six-year period. However, persons who were age 50 by January 1, 1986, may elect to have such amounts taxed at a flat 20 per cent capital gains rate. Tax Reform Act of 1986 §§1122(b)(1) and (h)(4).

At the end of the first full paragraph on page 296, insert:

The Tax Reform Act of 1986 (with limited exceptions for persons who attained age 50 before January 1, 1986) eliminated the 10-year averaging election and substituted 5-year averaging. Under the Act, persons who have not yet reached age 59 1/2 when they receive their lump sum distribution are prohibited from making any averaging election. I.R.C. §402(e)(1)(C).

At the end of the text on page 296, add:

With respect to a married participant in a qualified retirement plan, the Retirement Equity Act of 1984 generally requires that retirement benefits be paid in the form of a joint and survivor annuity for the participant and his or her spouse. Furthermore, the plan must provide that, if the participant dies prior to retirement, the death benefit be paid to the spouse in the form of a survivor annuity. The annuity payments to the spouse must be at least 50 per cent of the payments which would have been made to the participant if he or she had retired. Unless the spouse and the participant are married less than one year at the time the payments are to commence, these provisions cannot be waived without the spouse's consent. I.R.C. §§401(a)(11) and 417. The nonemployee spouse does not make a taxable gift by consenting to the waiver of such spouse's rights. I.R.C. §2503(f).

§13.17   ii. Estate Tax

Because §525 of the Deficit Reduction Act of 1984 eliminated the estate tax exclusion for death benefits payable under qualified retirement plans, and §1852(e) of the Tax Reform Act of 1986 repealed the estate tax exclusion for the community property interest of a non-employee spouse, the entire text on pages 296 and 297 is deleted.

§13.17A   (a) Penalty Tax on Excess Distributions (New)

The Tax Reform Act of 1986 imposes a 15 per cent excise tax to the extent that the aggregate distributions during one year, with limited exceptions, to a recipient from all exempt plans exceed $150,000. I.R.C. §4983. When distributions are received in a lump sum, up to $750,000 is exempt from this tax. I.R.C. §4983(c)(4). There is a special grandfather rule which, if elected, may shield even greater amounts from the excise tax. To elect to have the rule apply, the accrued benefit as of August 1, 1986 must exceed $562,500 and the election must be made on the employee's return for a taxable year ending before January 1, 1989. If the rule applies, the full amount of the accrued benefits as of August 1, 1986 will be excluded from the excise tax. However, if the rule is elected, amounts that accrue after August 1, 1986 will be subject to the 15 per cent tax. Moreover, if the election is made, and the employee receives periodic payments rather than a lump sum, the nongrandfathered amounts (determined on a pro-rata basis), are excludable to the extent of $112,500 per year, rather than $150,000 per year.

The Act also imposes a 15 per cent penalty tax, as an additional estate tax, upon the death of an individual whose estate or beneficiaries are entitled to receive in the aggregate an amount that exceeds the permitted exclusions. I.R.C. §4981(d)(1). The payment of the additional estate tax precludes any further imposition of the 15 per cent excise tax when the payments of the death benefit are actually made. It should be noted that this additional estate tax is payable even if the decedent's estate would otherwise not be subject to an estate tax. For example, neither the unified credit, the marital deduction, the charitable deduction, nor any other estate tax deductions are allowed in computing the 15 per cent penalty tax.

§13.18   iii. Gift Tax

Because §1852(e) of the Tax Reform Act of 1986 repealed the gift tax exclusion for gifts of an interest in a qualified retirement plan, the entire text on page 297 is deleted.

B.   Individual Plans

§13.19   1. Self-Employed Plans

At the end of the first paragraph on page 298 insert:

The Tax Equity and Fiscal Responsibility Act of 1982 generally eliminated the major distinctions which existed between corporate qualified plans and self-employed plans. The limits on defined contributions and defined benefit plans have been increased for taxable years beginning after December 31, 1983, to the permissible limits on corporate plans (see Supplement §13.14). §237 of The Tax Equity and Fiscal Responsibility Act of 1982.

§13.20   2. Individual Retirement Plans

The entire text on pages 297-298 is changed to read as follows:

The Tax Reform Act of 1986 substantially changed the rules applicable to the establishment of and contributions to an individual retirement account commonly called an "IRA." Whether or not an employee is covered by another corporate or self-employed plan, he may create an IRA and contribute to it annually to the extent of the lesser of $2,000 or 100 per cent of his earned income for the year. However, for the contribution to be deductible, the individual or, if a joint return is filed, the spouse may not be a participant in an employer-maintained qualified retirement plan, unless the adjusted gross income is under specified amounts. Single individuals must earn under $25,000 and couples under $40,000 for active participants to deduct their IRA contributions. However, if the single person has adjusted gross income between $25,000 and $35,000 and a married couple between $40,000 and $50,000, the deduction will be phased out ratably.

An additional $250 contribution for the benefit of a nonworking spouse may also be made annually. However, this contribution is only deductible to the extent that the earning spouse's contribution is deductible. I.R.C. §219(c).

Except for the limitation on contributions to an IRA plan and the fact that the averaging election (see §13.16) is not available to distributions, the income taxability of the benefits from such a plan are generally similar to a self-employed plan. (See §13.19.) Income from permitted nondeductible contributions is not taxable until distributed to the owner. Distributions from an IRA, whether the funds came from the taxpayers' contributions or from a "rollover" (see §13.16), must commence no later than age 70 1/2. Death benefits payable under an IRA are included in the decedent's estate for estate tax purposes.

§13.21   C. Estate Planning Considerations

The entire §13.21 on pages 299 through 301 is changed to read:

Because §525 of the Deficit Reduction Act of 1984 eliminated the estate tax exclusion for death benefits payable under qualified retirement plans, the estate planning considerations involved in payment of such benefits have been significantly altered.

The following considerations should be taken into account in order to properly coordinate the estate owner's interest in a qualified retirement plan with the estate plan (but before doing so, see Supplement §13.16 for a discussion of certain requirements regarding the method of payment of plan benefits):

1. When there is a surviving spouse to whom the estate owner desires to leave all or a portion of the estate, consider whether or not to designate the spouse (or a marital deduction trust, see §§4.14 to 4.24) as the death beneficary. The first point to consider is that whatever passes to the surviving spouse or to the marital deduction trust will later be included in the surviving spouse's estate. To the extent that the "equivalent" exemption is not otherwise utilized, serious thought should be given to designating all or part of the death benefit to a by-pass trust or to a nonspousal beneficiary. (See §4.8).

2. To the extent that the estate owner wishes to qualify all or part of the retirement plan death benefits for the marital deduction, an important reason exists for naming the spouse directly, rather than a marital deduction trust, as the primary beneficiary.

    Where a lump sum, or under certain circumstances at least 50 per cent of the distributable amount, is paid to a surviving spouse, the spouse may elect to "roll over" the distribution into an individual retirement account and thereby exclude such payment from income, except as distributions are then made from the IRA. When the surviving spouse dies, the proceeds payable from the IRA will be included in the surviving spouse's taxable estate. Reg. §20.2039-4(e).

When the estate owner's interest in the retirement plan is community property and the nonemployee spouse dies first, such spouse's one-half community property interest is included in the gross estate. To avoid estate tax, the nonemployee spouse should leave his or her interest to the other spouse in such a manner that it will qualify for the marital deduction. It would be advisable to leave this interest outright to the employee rather than to a marital deduction trust, the deductibility of which depends on the surviving spouse receiving current income, such as a "QTIP" trust. See §4.20. Particularly if the employee has not yet retired, no income will be payable from the plan and the marital deduction may be disallowed.

3. For income tax purposes, consider having the death benefit divided among as many recipients as possible, particularly if five-year averaging is not elected. The death benefits (less the deduction for the portion of the estate tax attributable to the death benefits) will be taxed as income in respect of a decedent (see §2.50). Therefore, by having the payments go to as many taxpayers as possible, the marginal income tax bracket may be lower. However, if one of the employee's beneficiaries is in a

particularly low income tax bracket, it may be advisable to have that person receive the entire death benefit and give items that are not taxed as income in respect of a decedent to the higher bracket recipients.

4.   Consider the designation of a charity as the recipient of the death benefit. When the payment goes to charity, income taxability will be avoided. The estate owner may then leave other assets that are not subject to income tax to noncharitable beneficiaries.

5.   Think about instituting a qualified retirement plan, particularly if the estate owner-employee is a major stockholder and would be a major participant in the plan. The plan will not only enable the stockholder to have sufficient funds for retirement, but having the security of a retirement plan will encourage the making of gifts of an interest in the business or gifts of other assets during his or her lifetime. These gifts, if properly made, can effectively reduce estate taxes. Despite the unification of estate and gift taxes mandated by the Tax Reform Act of 1976, the estate may still be reduced by the $10,000 annual exclusion portion of each gift (see §8.3), the future appreciation on the gifted asset (see §8.4), the amount of the gift tax paid on the gift (see §8.5), and the use of a grantor income trust (see Supplement §8.50). If not for the qualified retirement plan, the estate owner may be more concerned about providing for retirement, and may be reluctant to make gifts.

§13.22   VI. $5,000 Death Benefit Exclusion

At the end of the third sentence of the first paragraph on page 301 add:

The Tax Equity and Fiscal Responsibility Act of 1982 extends the $5,000 death benefit exclusion to a lump sum distribution from Keogh plans. I.R.C. §101(b)(3)(B).

VII.   Recommended Reading

Insert after Abdalla in the recommended reading list on page 301:

Adams and Hodgman, "Estate and Income Tax Planning for Qualified Retirement Benefits" 122 No 8 *Trusts and Estates* 38 (1983).

Insert after Bornstein in the recommended reading list on page 301:

Davis, "Allocating the $100,000 Exclusion" 10 *Estate Planning* 264 (1983).

Esterces, "Qualified Plan Benefits After DRA" 12 *Estate Planning* 80 (1985).

Frank, "Death Benefit Limitation Under TEFRA Requires Planning" 10 *Estate Planning* 2 (1983).

Hoyt, "Choosing Between Special 10 Year Averaging and Deferring Tax Through a Rollover" 60 *Journal of Taxation* 90 (1984).

Insert after Slavitt in the recommended reading list on page 302:

Sollee, "Top-Heavy Plans Under New Law" 57 *Journal of Taxation* 266 (1982).

Making Gifts to Charity 14

II. Income Tax Consequences of Outright Gifts

A. Cash Gifts

1. Maximum Income Tax Deduction—The Fifty Per Cent Rule

§14.5 b. Gifts to Private Foundations—The Twenty Per Cent Deduction Rule

The section title is changed to read:

§14.5 b. Gifts to Private Foundations—The Thirty Per Cent Rule

The second to last sentence of the text on page 306 is changed to read:

One such disincentive is that the ceiling on the deductibility of cash gifts to private foundations is only 30 per cent of the individual's contribution base.

§14.6 c. Interplay of the Fifty Per Cent and Twenty Per Cent Rules

The section title is changed to read:

§14.6 c. Interplay of the Fifty Per Cent and Thirty Per Cent Rules

The third sentence of the text on page 306 is changed to read:

If gifts to "public" charities total less than 50 per cent of the taxpayer's contribution base, then contributions to private foundations (up to the 30 per cent limit) may be used to make up the 50 per cent maximum total deduction allowed.

§14.7 2. Carryover of Excess Contributions

The first sentence of the first paragraph on page 306 is changed to read:

In the case of all charities, cash contributions in excess of the maximum deductible amount of the contribution base may be carried forward and deducted over the five years following the contribution.

The last paragraph on page 307 is deleted.

§14.8 B. Gifts of Noncash Property

At the end of the text on page 307, add:

The Deficit Reduction Act of 1984 increases the penalty for overvaluing property contributed to charity and requires the Treasury Department to adopt regulations necessitating appraisals, under certain conditions, for contributions of noncash property. See §155 of the Act; I.R.C. §170 and 6050L.

§14.9 1. Ordinary Income Property

The last sentence of the third paragraph on page 307 is changed to read:

In short, there is a 50 per cent ceiling for gifts to "public" charities, with a five-year carryover for the excess, and a 30 per cent limit on gifts to private foundations, with no carryover allowed.

§14.10   2. Capital Gain Property

The following sentence is inserted between the second and third sentences of the first paragraph on page 307:

However, if the asset is purchased after June 22, 1984, but before January 1, 1988, the holding period for long-term capital gain or loss is more than six months, rather than more than one year.

§14.11   a. Gifts to Private Foundations

The entire text is changed to read as follows:

If capital gain property is given to a private foundation (see §14.5), the amount deductible is equal to the fair market value of the property reduced by 100 per cent of the appreciation. I.R.C. §170(e)(1)(B)(ii). For example, assume that a taxpayer contributes real estate he has held for more than one year to a private foundation. The property cost $10,000 and is worth $26,000 when given to charity. The amount deductible is $10,000.

There is, however, an exception for appreciated stock of a corporation for which market quotations are readily available on an established securities market. The full fair market value of such stock contributed prior to January 1, 1995, is deductible. In order to obtain the full deduction, however, neither the donor nor members of the donor's family (as defined in I.R.C. §267(c)(4)) may have in the aggregate contributed more than 10 per cent of the outstanding stock of the corporation to any private foundation. I.R.C. §170(e)(5).

The contribution base ceiling on all gifts of appreciated property to a private foundation is the lesser of (1) 20 per cent of the contribution base, or (2) the excess up to 50 per cent of the contribution base over the amount of charitable contributions qualifying for the 50 per cent deduction limitation. (See §§14.5 and 14.6.)

§14.12   b. Gifts to "Public" Charities

The citation prior to the last sentence of the first paragraph on page 308 is changed to read as follows:

I.R.C. §170(b)(1)(C).

§14.13   i. Special Election Available

The reference in the second sentence on page 308 to 40 per cent is changed to read:

100 per cent

The citation at the end of the second sentence on page 308 is changed to read:

I.R.C. §170(b)(1)(C)(iii).

The last sentence on page 309 is changed to read as follows:

If he makes the election, he can deduct a total of $20,000 in the current year, with no carryover.

§14.14   ii. Gifts of Tangible Personal Property Unrelated to the Charity's Functions

The first paragraph on page 309 is changed to read as follows:

If the "public" charity does not, and cannot reasonably be expected to, use a gift of tangible personal property in a manner related to its functions and activities, the deduction is reduced by 100 per cent of the capital gain which would have arisen if the property had been sold. I.R.C. §170(e)(1)(B)(i). Thus, the taxpayer may only deduct the cost basis of the property. The percentage limits on deducting such gifts are the same as those for cash gifts to "public" charities, namely 50 per cent of the donor's contribution base. (See §14.3.) As an example, a taxpayer contributes a capital gain painting to a hospital. The painting cost $1,000 and is worth $2,000 when donated. The hospital sells the painting and uses the proceeds to purchase medical supplies. The amount deductible is $1,000.

§14.15   3. Carryover of Excess Contributions of Appreciated Assets

The entire text is changed to read as follows:

Any excess capital gain property contributed may be carried over as a contribution into the next five years. (See I.R.C. §§170(b)(1)(C)(ii) and (D)(ii).) However, the carryover will be subject to the 30 per cent ceiling in each of the succeeding five years (see §14.12) unless, in the case of a public charity, the special election is made. Under this election the taxpayer may apply the 50 per cent ceiling, but his total deduction will be limited to the cost basis of the property, thereby decreasing the amount left to be carried over. (See §14.13.)

§14.16   4. Tax Advantage of Gifts of Appreciated Capital Gain Property

The entire text is changed to read as follows:

Contributions of appreciated long-term capital gain property may result in substantial tax savings when compared to gifts of cash or other assets. With the exception of "unrelated use" tangible personal property (discussed in §14.14), the donor may deduct the full market value of the property (up to the maximum limits of adjusted gross income) given to a "public" charity and yet pay no capital gain tax on the appreciation. A gift of the appreciated property, as is illustrated in the following example, may therefore be made at a lower cost than if the property were sold and the cash proceeds contributed. Assume that A is in a 28 per cent tax bracket. He owns capital gain securities which cost $1,000 and now have a value of $10,000. A contribution of the securities to a "public" charity will result in a $10,000 deduction for income tax purposes (subject to the special election discussed in §14.13) and, hence, a tax savings of $2,800, or a net after-tax cost of $7,200 ($10,000 [value of securities] minus $2,800 [tax savings]). On the other hand, if A desires to contribute cash and thereby sells the securities to raise such cash or to replenish cash which he otherwise uses, his net after-tax cost of the charitable contribution will be greater. If he sells the securities for $10,000, he will have to pay a capital gains tax of $2,520 so that his net after-tax cost will be $9,720 ($10,000 [value of securities] plus $2,520 [capital gains tax] minus $2,800 [tax savings]).

The Tax Reform Act of 1986 treats the amount of appreciation in contributed capital gain property as a preference item in computing the alternative minimum tax. I.R.C. §57(a)(6). If the estate owner is subject to the alternative minimum tax, he should take this into account before making gifts of appreciated capital gain property to a charity.

§14.17   5. Bargain Sales of Appreciated Capital Gain Property to Charity

The fourth sentence of the last paragraph on page 311 is changed to read:

This rule applies to a gift of encumbered property regardless of whether or not the charity assumes the liability, Reg. §1.1011-2(b)(3), whether or not the liability is with or without recourse, *Guest v Commr*

77 TC 9 (1981), and whether or not the fair market value of the property is less than the amount of the liability. *Commr v Tufts* 456 US 960, 103 SCt 1826 (1983).

IV.   Gifts of Split Interests in Trust

B.   Charitable Remainder Trusts

1.   Annuity Trust and Unitrust

§14.24   a. Annuity Trust

At the end of the second paragraph on page 314 add:

Because of new valuation tables (see Appendix VIII of the Supplement for explanation), new calculations should be substituted in the example in the text. In the example, the annuity factor at age 50, for either a male or a female, is now 8.4743. (See Supplement Appendix VIII, Table A.) The present value of the yearly payout is $42,372 ($5,000 times 8.4743) and the remainder interest would, therefore, be $57,628, which amount is deductible for tax purposes.

§14.25   b. Unitrust

Because of new valuation tables appearing in Reg. §1.664-4, the last sentence of the fourth paragraph on page 315 is changed to read:

In the above example, whether the estate owner is a male or a female, age 50, the value of the remainder interest for tax deduction purposes under either type of unitrust is $31,874.

§14.33   3. Estate Planning Advantages of Charitable Remainder Trusts

At the end of the text on page 319, add:

The charitable remainder trust, in certain instances, may even be used to advantage when the married estate owner wishes not only to provide for a surviving spouse, but also for children on the surviving spouse's death. By creating a charitable remainder trust during his or her lifetime, the estate owner will generate an income tax deduction in an amount equal to the value of the remainder going to charity. The tax savings resulting from this deduction can then be used, in whole or in part, to purchase life insurance on one or both of the lives of the spouses in a face amount which will replace for the children the value of what will go to the charity on the surviving spouse's death. This life insurance can be placed in an irrevocable life insurance trust designed to exclude the life insurance proceeds from the estates of both spouses. See §§10.49 and 10.50. Because of this exclusion, the net amount going to the children when the surviving spouse dies could be much larger than would otherwise have been the case if the assets placed in the charitable remainder trust had otherwise gone to the children, but had first been taxable in the surviving spouse's estate.

V. Gifts of Charitable Income Interest

§14.35 A. Income Tax Consequences of Charitable Lead Trusts

The third sentence of the first paragraph on page 320 is changed to read:

This would be the case if, for example, the donor's reversionary interest exceeds 5 per cent of the value of the transfer to the trust.

The last sentence of the second paragraph on page 320 is changed to read as follows:

Since the estate owner, in order to obtain the charitable deduction, must pay income tax on the income earned by the trust, a charitable lead trust is seldom created by the estate owner during lifetime.

§14.36 B. Estate and Gift Tax Consequences of Charitable Lead Trusts

At the end of the text on page 321 add:

Because of new valuation tables (see Appendix VIII of the Supplement for explanation), new calculations should be substituted in the example in the text. The new tables are predicated on a 10 per cent interest factor. Accordingly, a charitable lead trust has lost some of its appeal. In the example in the text, the estate tax deduction will be only $426,204 ($60,000 times 7.1034, see Supplement Appendix VIII, Table B), rather than $500,000. In order to deduct the full $500,000, the annuity payment period would have to last for at least 19 years.

VII. Recommended Reading

Insert after Ashby in the recommended reading list on page 321:

Gilbert and Waldman, "When to Use Private Foundations to Best Advantage" 12 *Estate Planning* 212 (1985).

Insert after Sorlien and Olsen in the recommended reading list on page 321:

Sweet, "The Economics of the Charitable Lead Trust" 122 No 10 *Trusts and Estates* 12 (1983).

Tax Planning the Estate After the Owner's Death

15

§15.4 III. Making an Analysis of the Estate

Immediately following Item 6 on page 326 add:

7.   Ascertain whether any of the beneficiaries are willing to make disclaimers, if there are tax savings by doing so.

IV. Elections Available to the Executor

A. Decedent's Final Income Tax Return (Form 1040)

1. Should the Estate File a Joint Return with the Surviving Spouse?

a. Advantages of Joint Return

§15.8 i. Planning to Take Advantage of Joint Return

The second sentence on page 327 is changed to read:

When the surviving spouse files a joint return, this income may be taxed at a lower effective rate than if it had remained in the estate and had been taxed accordingly.

§15.10   2. Medical Deduction Election

At the end of the first sentence in the first paragraph on page 328, delete I.R.C. citation and replace with:

I.R.C. §213(c)(1)

At the end of the second sentence in the first paragraph on page 328, delete I.R.C. citation and replace with:

I.R.C. §213(c)(2)

The first sentence of the second paragraph on page 328 (including the citation) is changed to read:

The income tax deduction is limited to medical expenses in excess of 7.5 per cent of adjusted gross income. I.R.C. §213(a)

C.   Deduction Election for Administration Expenses and Losses

§15.15   1. Disallowance of Double Deductions

At the end of the second paragraph on page 331, insert:

The Tax Reform Act of 1986 generally subjects miscellaneous (below-the-line) deductions to a floor of 2 per cent of adjusted gross income, so these expenses may be deducted only to the extent that the 2 per cent floor is exceeded. I.R.C. §67. However, in the case of an estate or trust, administration expenses *which would not have been incurred if the property were not held in the estate or trust* are not subject to the 2 per cent floor. I.R.C. §67(e). Some administration expenses, as for example, investment advisory fees, may have been incurred even if the property were not held by the estate or trust. Accordingly, the executor should consider deducting that type of expense on the estate tax return in order to obtain a greater benefit.

At the end of the last paragraph on page 331 add:

Estate of Bailly v Commr 81 TC 246 (1983); see also Rev. Rul. 84-75, 1984-1 C.B. 193.

Under the Tax Reform Act of 1986, interest paid on a §6166 (closely held business) tax deferral or a §6163 (reversionary or remainder interest) tax deferral may be deducted on the estate income tax return if the executor so elects. See Supplement §12.52. However, all other interest paid by an estate on tax deficiencies is not deductible on the income tax return. I.R.C. §163(h). Accordingly, the executor should deduct such other interest payments on the estate tax return.

§15.16   2. Manner of Making the Election

At the end of the text on page 331 add:

In order to prevent estates from claiming the same deductions on both the estate tax return and the income tax return and then neglecting to file the waiver prior to the expiration of the statutory period of limitations, the Treasury Department has issued proposed regulations that impose a time limit for filing the waiver. If the items are claimed as income tax deductions, the waiver will have to be filed with the income tax return. If, prior to the filing of the income tax return, the items are used to reduce the estate tax, the waiver must be filed at least 180 days before the expiration of the statutory period of limitations in regard to the estate tax. See proposed Reg. §1.642(g)-1(a)(2).

§15.26   D. "QTIP" Election

The last two sentences on page 335 are deleted, and the following is inserted:

Under proposed regulations, the executor may, if he wishes, elect to deduct only a portion of the bequest left to a "QTIP" trust. Proposed Reg. §20.2056(b)-7(b). However, such partial election must relate to a fractional or percentile share of the property as opposed to a fixed dollar amount. The fractional or percentile share may be defined by means of a formula. As a result, the executor, for example, should be able to limit the election to only that portion of the "QTIP" trust assets which will eliminate the federal estate tax after applying the other deductions and credits to which the estate is entitled. Letter Rul. 8301050.

§15.27   E. Election of Alternate Valuation Date

At the end of the first paragraph on page 335, add:

For decedents dying after July 18, 1984, the alternate valuation date may be elected only if the election will both reduce the value of the gross estate and decrease the estate tax. The purpose of this requirement is to prevent the estate from increasing the income tax basis of the estate assets when there is no federal estate tax payable, as would be the case when there is a surviving spouse and a maximum or optimum marital deduction has been used. See §4.8.

At the end of the third paragraph on page 335 insert:

The Technical Corrections Act of 1982 permits the use of a fast write-off of inherited depreciable property under the accelerated cost recovery system. I.R.C. §168(e)(4)(H).

The fourth and fifth paragraphs on pages 335 and 336 are deleted and in place thereof the following two paragraphs are inserted:

Even when an optimum marital deduction bequest is used, as will be seen, it may be possible to elect the alternate valuation date when the value of the estate is lower on that date. By having lower values, a lesser amount will generally pass into the marital bequest and thereby reduce the estate tax on the surviving spouse's death. To illustrate, assume the date of death value of the estate is $2,000,000, the alternate value is $1,800,000, and a pecuniary marital deduction bequest (see §4.30) is used. Also assume that, other than the marital deduction and the unified credit, there are no other deductions or credits available and the first spouse to die dies after 1986. If the date of death valuation is selected, $1,400,000 will be allocated to the marital bequest; whereas if the alternate valuation date is used, only $1,200,000 will pass into the marital deduction portion. If a fractional share marital deduction bequest is used, 14/20ths of each asset would be allocated to the marital bequest, based on date of death values, but only 12/18ths of each asset, when based on alternate date values. Before making a final decision, the executor must weigh the potential savings of estate tax in the surviving spouse's estate against the lower income tax basis of the assets held by the estate of the first spouse to die.

In order to make the alternate valuation date election, not only must the gross estate be reduced thereby, but the estate tax must also be lessened. I.R.C. §2032(c). If there is no estate tax payable, obviously this requirement cannot be satisfied. A small estate tax can, however, be "created" by the executor making only a partial "QTIP" election (see §15.26) or by having the surviving spouse disclaim a portion of the marital deduction bequest (see §15.39).

The last paragraph on page 336 is changed to read:

To deter anyone from deliberately overvaluing an asset in order to obtain a higher income tax basis, I.R.C. §6659 subjects a taxpayer who uses an overvaluation for income tax purposes to a tax penalty. The penalty applies when an estate beneficiary adopts an overstated amount shown on the federal estate tax return as his or her income tax basis. Rev. Rul. 85-75, I.R.B. 1985-23, 19. This penalty is assessed under the following circumstances:

1. The property was held by the taxpayer for less than five years
2. The underpayment of income tax attributable to the overstatement of value is at least $1,000
3. There was no reasonable basis for the valuation claimed on the return

The penalty is a percentage of the underpayment, computed as follows:

Claimed Valuation as a Percentage of Correct Valuation	Penalty Percentage
Under 150 per cent	0
150 per cent to 200 per cent	10
200 per cent to 250 per cent	20
more than 250 per cent	30

V. Distribution Planning

B. Objectives of Distribution Planning

1. Equalize Tax Rates

§15.33 a. Family Allowance

The second sentence on page 338 is changed to read:

Such an award is deemed to be an income item (to the extent the estate received net income), even if paid out of principal.

2. Maximize Deductions

§15.36 c. Excess Deductions

At the end of the text on page 339, add:

Under the Tax Reform Act of 1986, excess deductions on the beneficiary's return are subject to the 2 per cent floor regarding itemized miscellaneous deductions. I.R.C. §67. See Supplement §15.15 for an explanation of the floor.

§15.37   3. Create Additional Taxpayers by Use of Trusts

The following is added at the end of the text on page 340:

The Tax Reform Act of 1986 requires trusts to use a calendar year. I.R.C. §645. Hence, deferring the taxation of income to the beneficiary by the use of a trust fiscal year will no longer be possible.

VI.   Disclaimers

§15.38   A. Introduction

The first sentence of the second paragraph on page 340 is changed to read:

In order to avoid any gift tax and also to prevent the disclaimed inherited asset from increasing B's estate, the disclaimer must not be deemed to constitute a taxable gift from B to his children.

At the end of the first full paragraph on page 341 delete the citation and add:

See Reg. §25.2518-2(e)(2) example (5). But see Letter Rul. 8509092, which indicates that where the disclaiming beneficiary is the trustee of the trust into which the disclaimed assets pass, a discretionary fiduciary power to appoint limited by an ascertainable standard is allowed.

The last paragraph on page 341 is deleted and in place thereof the following is inserted:

The regulations, with limited exceptions, treat the interest of a joint tenant as a completed irrevocable gift on the date the tenancy was created. Reg. §25.2518-2(c)(4)(i). Hence, the surviving joint tenant must file a qualified disclaimer no later than nine months after the establishment of the joint tenancy, rather than nine months from the death of the deceased joint tenant. One of the stated exceptions deals with joint tenancy bank accounts. Within nine months from the decedent's death, the surviving joint tenant may disclaim that portion of the account attributable to the decedent's contributions. (See Reg. §25.2518-2(c)(5) example (9)). One court of appeals carved out an even broader exception. In *Kennedy v Commr* __ F2d __ (7th Cir 1986)

(86-2 USTC ¶13,699), the court held that when either joint tenant under state law is allowed to partition the joint tenancy asset, the surviving joint tenant has nine months from the decedent's death to disclaim the decedent's one-half interest.

A disclaimer of a partial interest may be made of an undivided portion of an asset and also of a separate interest in property. Reg. §25.2518-3. For example, one can disclaim a fractional portion of a bequest or, if he is left an income interest in property, he can disclaim all or a fractional portion of the income interest. He may also disclaim an interest in principal, such as limited power to invade, without disclaiming the income interest. A specific asset in a trust may be disclaimed only if that asset is removed from the trust. Reg. §25.2518-3(a)(2). Similarly, a disclaimer of a pecuniary amount from a bequest is effective only if the disclaimed amount is segregated from the remaining portion of the bequest. Reg. §25.2518-3(c). One of the purposes of these requirements is to prevent the disclaiming party from receiving any benefit from the disclaimed interests.

B. Additional Factors to Be Considered

§15.40   2. Powers of Appointment

The last sentence on page 342 is deleted and the following is inserted in place thereof:

A testamentary power of appointment is treated as a separate interest in property. Accordingly, the power may be disclaimed even though the disclaiming party retains the additional right to invade principal under an ascertainable standard. However, he must also disclaim any other power over principal which is not limited to an ascertainable standard, such as a lifetime power to make gifts to third persons. If such other nonascertainable power is not disclaimed, the disclaimer of the general testamentary power will not be effective. Reg. §25.2518-3(a)(iii).

VII.   Recommended Reading

Insert after Ferguson in the recommended reading list on page 343:

Kasner, *Post Mortem Tax Planning* (Shepard's/McGraw-Hill 1982, currently supplemented).

Insert after Lyons in the recommended reading list on page 343:

Reisman and Green, "Pass Through of Excess Losses and Credits" 10
   Estate Planning 194 (1983).

Appendixes

I. TABLE I: FEDERAL INDIVIDUAL INCOME TAX
               RATES

Table I on pages 345 through 347 of the text is deleted and the following is inserted:

1. Married Filing a Joint Return (and qualified surviving spouse)

Tax Years Beginning in 1987

Taxable Income	Tax on Left Column	Tax Rate On Excess
-0-	-0-	11%
3,000	330	15%
28,000	4,080	28%
45,000	8,840	35%
90,000	24,590	38.5%

Maximum 1987 long-term capital gain rate is 28%

Tax Years Beginning in 1988

Taxable Income	Tax on Left Column	Tax Rate On Excess
-0-	-0-	15%
28,750	4,462.50	28%
71,900	16,264.50	33%
149,250*	41,790.00	28%

*The $149,250 "top of the 33% bracket" amount in 1988 is increased by $10,920 per personal exemption (the 33% tax on which is $3,603.60).

2. Head of Household

Tax Years Beginning in 1987

Taxable Income	Tax on Left Column	Tax Rate On Excess
-0-	-0-	11%
2,500	275	15%
23,000	3,350	28%
38,000	7,550	35%
80,000	22,250	38.5%

Maximum 1987 long-term capital gain rate is 28%

Tax Years Beginning in 1988

Taxable Income	Tax on Left Column	Tax Rate On Excess
-0-	-0-	15%
23,900	3,585.00	28%
61,650	14,155.00	33%
123,790*	34,661.20	28%

*The $123,790 "top of the 33% bracket" amount in 1988 is increased by $10,920 per personal exemption (the 33% tax on which is $3,603.60).

3. Single Individual

Note—unearned income over $1,000 of a child under age 14 at year end is taxed at parental top rates (if higher).

Tax Years Beginning in 1987

Taxable Income	Tax on Left Column	Tax Rate On Excess
-0-	-0-	11%
1,800	198	15%
16,800	2,448	28%
27,000	5,304	35%
54,000	14,754	38.5%

Maximum 1987 long-term capital gain rate is 28%

Tax Years Beginning in 1988

Taxable Income	Tax on Left Column	Tax Rate On Excess
-0-	-0-	15%
17,850	2,677.50	28%
43,150	9,761.50	33%
89,560*	25,076.80	28%

*The $89,560 "top of the 33% bracket" amount in 1988 is increased by $10,920 per personal exemption (the 33% tax on which is $3,603.60).

4. Married Filing a Separate Return

Tax Years Beginning in 1987

Taxable Income	Tax on Left Column	Tax Rate On Excess
-0-	-0-	11%
1,500	165	15%
14,000	2,040	28%
22,500	4,420	35%
45,000	12,295	38.5%

Maximum 1987 long-term capital gain rate is 28%

Tax Years Beginning in 1988

Taxable Income	Tax on Left Column	Tax Rate On Excess
-0-	-0-	15%
14,875	2,231.25	28%
35,950	8,132.25	33%
113,300*	33,657.75	28%

*The $113,300 "top of the 33% bracket" amount in 1988 is increased by $10,920 per personal exemption (the 33% tax on which is 3,603.60).

5. Trusts and Estates

Tax Years Beginning in 1987

Taxable Income	Tax on Left Column	Tax Rate On Excess
-0-	-0-	11%
500	55	15%
4,700	685	28%
7,550	1,483	35%
15,150	4,143	38.5%

Maximum 1987 long-term capital gain rate is 28%

Tax Years Beginning in 1988

Taxable Income	Tax on Left Column	Tax Rate On Excess
-0-	-0-	15%
5,000	750	28%
13,000	2,990	33%
26,000	7,280	28%

II.   TABLE II: FEDERAL UNIFIED TRANSFER TAX RATES

C.   1984

The heading of this table, appearing on page 350, should be changed to read:

C.   1984–1988 Inclusive

D.   1985 and thereafter

The heading of this table, appearing on page 351, should be changed to read:

D.   1988 and thereafter

V.   TABLE V: CALIFORNIA INHERITANCE AND
GIFT TAX RATES AND EXEMPTIONS

At the bottom of Table V on page 354 add:

California, by a voters' initiative, repealed its inheritance and gift tax effective June 9, 1982. However, it retained an estate tax equal to the maximum credit for state death taxes allowable in computing the federal estate tax (i.e. the pick-up tax, see §2.34).

VIII.   TABLE VIII: VALUATIONS OF ANNUITIES;
LIFE ESTATES AND REMAINDERS
(Reg §20.2031-10)

TABLE B

The third columnar heading of Table VIII B appearing on page 365 should read **"Term Certain"** *instead of* **"Life Estate."**

At the end of Table VIII B on page 365 add:

The Treasury Department adopted regulations containing tables which replace the valuation tables valuing annuities, life estates, income term interests, and remainder interests set forth in Table VIII of the Appendix to the Text. Reg. §§20.2031-7(f) and 25.2512-5. The new tables are effective retroactively to December 1, 1983.

The new tables are set forth below. They are unisex tables, so there is no longer a distinction for valuation purposes between males and females. The new tables are constructed by using an internal interest rate of 10 per cent, compared to the 6 per cent interest rate which was used in the old tables. Accordingly, annuities, life estates, and income term interests have become more valuable and remainder interests less valuable.

The reader is cautioned to consider the effect of the new tables in planning all transactions involving the use of valuation tables.

TABLE A

Single life, unisex, 10 percent showing the present worth of an annuity, of a life interest, and of a remainder interest

1 Age	2 Annuity	3 Life Estate	4 Remainder	1 Age	2 Annuity	3 Life Estate	4 Remainder
0	9.7188	.97188	.02812	43	8.9855	.89855	.10145
1	9.8988	.98988	.01012	44	8.9221	.89221	.10779
2	9.9017	.99017	.00983	45	8.8558	.88558	.11442
3	9.9008	.99008	.00992	46	8.7863	.87863	.12137
4	9.8981	.98981	.01019	47	8.7137	.87137	.12863
5	9.8938	.98938	.01062	48	8.6374	.86374	.13626
6	9.8884	.98884	.01116	49	8.5578	.85578	.14422
7	9.8822	.98822	.01178	50	8.4743	.84743	.15257
8	9.8748	.98748	.01252	51	8.3874	.83874	.16126
9	9.8663	.98663	.01337	52	8.2969	.82969	.17031
10	9.8565	.98565	.01435	53	8.2028	.82028	.17972
11	9.8453	.98453	.01547	54	8.1054	.81054	.18946
12	9.8329	.98329	.01671	55	8.0046	.80046	.19954
13	9.8198	.98198	.01802	56	7.9006	.79006	.20994
14	9.8066	.98066	.01934	57	7.7931	.77931	.22069
15	9.7937	.97937	.02063	58	7.6822	.76822	.23178
16	9.7815	.97815	.02185	59	7.5675	.75675	.24325
17	9.7700	.97700	.02300	60	7.4491	.74491	.25509
18	9.7590	.97590	.02410	61	7.3267	.73267	.26733
19	9.7480	.97480	.02520	62	7.2002	.72002	.27998
20	9.7365	.97365	.02635	63	7.0696	.70696	.29304
21	9.7245	.97245	.02755	64	6.9352	.69352	.30648
22	9.7120	.97120	.02880	65	6.7970	.67970	.32030
23	9.6986	.96986	.03014	66	6.6551	.66551	.33449
24	9.6841	.96841	.03159	67	6.5098	.65098	.34902
25	9.6678	.96678	.03322	68	6.3610	.63610	.36390
26	9.6495	.96495	.03505	69	6.2086	.62086	.37914
27	9.6290	.96290	.03710	70	6.0522	.60522	.39478
28	9.6062	.96062	.03938	71	5.8914	.58914	.41086
29	9.5813	.95813	.04187	72	5.7261	.57261	.42739
30	9.5543	.95543	.04457	73	5.5571	.55571	.44429
31	9.5254	.95254	.04746	74	5.3862	.53862	.46138
32	9.4942	.94942	.05058	75	5.2149	.52149	.47851
33	9.4608	.94608	.05392	76	5.0441	.50441	.49559
34	9.4250	.94250	.05750	77	4.8742	.48742	.51258
35	9.3868	.93868	.06132	78	4.7049	.47049	.52951
36	9.3460	.93460	.06540	79	4.5357	.45357	.54643
37	9.3026	.93026	.06974	80	4.3659	.43659	.56341
38	9.2567	.92567	.07433	81	4.1967	.41967	.58033
39	9.2083	.92083	.07917	82	4.0295	.40295	.59705
40	9.1571	.91571	.08429	83	3.8642	.38642	.61358
41	9.1030	.91030	.08970	84	3.6998	.36998	.63002
42	9.0457	.90457	.09543				

TABLE A (*continued*)
Single life, unisex, 10 percent showing the present worth of an annuity, of a life interest, and of a remainder interest

1 Age	2 Annuity	3 Life Estate	4 Remainder	1 Age	2 Annuity	3 Life Estate	4 Remainder
85	3.5359	.35359	.64641	98	2.1000	.21000	.79000
86	3.3764	.33764	.66236	99	2.0486	.20486	.79514
87	3.2262	.32262	.67738	100	1.9975	.19975	.80025
88	3.0859	.30859	.69141	101	1.9532	.19532	.80468
89	2.9526	.29526	.70474	102	1.9054	.19054	.80946
90	2.8221	.28221	.71779	103	1.8437	.18437	.81563
91	2.6955	.26955	.73045	104	1.7856	.17856	.82144
92	2.5771	.25771	.74229	105	1.6962	.16962	.83038
93	2.4692	.24692	.75308	106	1.5488	.15488	.84512
94	2.3728	.23728	.76272	107	1.3409	.13409	.86591
95	2.2887	.22887	.77113	108	1.0068	.10068	.89932
96	2.2181	.22181	.77819	109	.4545	.04545	.95455
97	2.1550	.21550	.78450				

TABLE B

Table showing the present worth at 10 per cent of an annuity for a term certain of an income interest for a term certain, and of a remainder interest postponed for a term certain

1 Number of Years	2 Annuity	3 Term Certain	4 Remainder	1 Number of Years	2 Annuity	3 Term Certain	4 Remainder
1	.9091	.090909	.909091	31	9.4790	.947901	.052099
2	1.7355	.173554	.826446	32	9.5264	.952638	.047362
3	2.4869	.248685	.751315	33	9.5694	.956943	.043057
4	3.1699	.316987	.683013	34	9.6086	.960857	.039143
5	3.7908	.379079	.620921	35	9.6442	.964416	.035584
6	4.3553	.435526	.564474	36	9.6765	.967651	.032349
7	4.8684	.486842	.513158	37	9.7059	.970592	.029408
8	5.3349	.533493	.466507	38	9.7327	.973265	.026735
9	5.7590	.575902	.424098	39	9.7570	.975696	.024304
10	6.1446	.614457	.385543	40	9.7791	.977905	.022095
11	6.4951	.649506	.350494	41	9.7991	.979914	.020086
12	6.8137	.681369	.318631	42	9.8174	.981740	.018260
13	7.1034	.710336	.289664	43	9.8340	.983400	.016600
14	7.3667	.736669	.263331	44	9.8491	.984909	.015091
15	7.6061	.760608	.238392	45	9.8628	.986281	.013719
16	7.8237	.782371	.217629	46	9.8753	.987528	.012472
17	8.0216	.802155	.197845	47	9.8866	.988662	.011338
18	8.2014	.820141	.179859	48	9.8969	.989693	.010307
19	8.3649	.836492	.163508	49	9.9063	.990630	.009370
20	8.5136	.851356	.148644	50	9.9148	.991481	.008519
21	8.6487	.864869	.135131	51	9.9226	.992256	.007744
22	8.7715	.877154	.122846	52	9.9296	.992960	.007040
23	8.8832	.888322	.111678	53	9.9360	.993600	.006400
24	8.9847	.898474	.101526	54	9.9418	.994182	.005818
25	9.0770	.907704	.092296	55	9.9471	.994711	.005289
26	9.1609	.916095	.083905	56	9.9519	.995191	.004809
27	9.2372	.923722	.076278	57	9.9563	.995629	.004371
28	9.3066	.930657	.069343	58	9.9603	.996026	.003974
29	9.3696	.936961	.063039	59	9.9639	.996387	.003613
30	9.4269	.942691	.057309	60	9.9672	.996716	.003284

Table IX on page 366 should read as follows:

IX.   TABLE IX: ORDINARY LIFE ANNUITIES—ONE LIFE—EXPECTED RETURN MULTIPLES (Reg. §1.72-9)

Ordinary Life Annuities—One Life—Expected Return Multiples

Ages		Multiples	Ages		Multiples	Ages		Multiples
Male	Female		Male	Female		Male	Female	
6	11	65.0	31	36	41.9	56	61	21.0
7	12	64.1	32	37	41.0	57	62	20.3
8	13	63.2	33	38	40.0	58	63	19.6
9	14	62.3	34	39	39.1	59	64	18.9
10	15	61.4	35	40	38.2	60	65	18.2
11	16	60.4	36	41	37.3	61	66	17.5
12	17	59.5	37	42	36.5	62	67	16.9
13	18	58.6	38	43	35.6	63	68	16.2
14	19	57.7	39	44	34.7	64	69	15.6
15	20	56.7	40	45	33.8	65	70	15.0
16	21	55.3	41	46	33.0	66	71	14.4
17	22	54.9	42	47	32.1	67	72	13.8
18	23	53.9	43	48	31.2	68	73	13.2
19	24	53.0	44	49	30.4	69	74	12.6
20	25	52.1	45	50	29.6	70	75	12.1
21	26	51.1	46	51	23.7	71	76	11.6
22	27	50.2	47	52	27.9	72	77	11.0
23	28	49.3	48	53	27.1	73	78	10.5
24	29	48.3	49	54	26.3	74	79	10.1
25	30	47.4	50	55	25.5	75	80	9.6
26	31	46.5	51	56	24.7	76	81	9.1
27	32	45.6	52	57	24.0	77	82	8.7
28	33	44.6	53	58	23.2	78	83	8.3
29	34	43.7	54	59	22.4	79	84	7.8
30	35	42.8	55	60	21.7	80	85	7.5

TABLE IX (*continued*)

Ages		Multiples	Ages		Multiples	Ages		Multiples
Male	Female		Male	Female		Male	Female	
81	86	7.1	91	96	4.0	101	106	1.9
82	87	6.7	92	97	3.7	102	107	1.7
83	88	6.3	93	98	3.5	103	108	1.5
84	89	6.0	94	99	3.3	104	109	1.3
85	90	5.7	95	100	3.1	105	110	1.2
86	91	5.4	96	101	2.9	106	111	1.0
87	92	5.1	97	102	2.7	107	112	.8
88	93	4.8	98	103	2.5	108	113	.7
89	94	4.5	99	104	2.3	109	114	.6
90	95	4.2	100	105	2.1	110	115	.3
						111	116	0

The following sex neutral table should be used for valuing annuities purchased after June 30, 1986:

Table IX.A

Ordinary Life Annuities—One Life—Expected Return Multiples

Age	Multiple	Age	Multiple
5	76.6	40	42.5
6	75.6	41	41.5
7	74.7	42	40.6
8	73.7	43	39.6
9	72.7	44	38.7
10	71.7	45	37.7
11	70.7	46	36.8
12	69.7	47	35.9
13	68.8	48	34.9
14	67.8	49	34.0
15	66.8	50	33.1
16	65.8	51	32.2
17	64.8	52	31.3
18	63.9	53	30.4
19	62.9	54	29.5
20	61.9	55	28.6
21	60.9	56	27.7
22	59.9	57	26.8
23	59.9	58	25.9
24	58.9	59	25.0
25	57.9	60	24.2
26	56.0	61	23.3
27	55.1	62	22.5
28	54.1	63	21.6
29	53.1	64	20.8
30	52.2	65	20.0
31	51.2	66	19.2
32	50.2	67	18.4
33	49.3	68	17.6
34	48.3	69	16.8
35	47.3	70	16.0
36	46.4	71	15.3
37	45.4	72	14.6
38	44.4	73	13.9
39	43.5	74	13.2

Table IX.A (*continued*)

Age	Multiple	Age	Multiple
75	12.5	96	3.4
76	11.9	97	3.2
77	11.2	98	3.0
78	10.6	99	2.8
79	10.0	100	2.7
80	9.5	101	2.5
81	8.9	102	2.3
82	8.4	103	2.1
83	7.9	104	1.9
84	7.4	105	1.8
85	6.9	106	1.6
86	6.5	107	1.4
87	6.1	108	1.3
88	5.7	109	1.1
89	5.3	110	1.0
90	5.0	111	.9
91	4.7	112	.8
92	4.4	113	.7
93	4.1	114	.6
94	3.9	115	.5
95	3.7		

Statutes (IRC)

1(f) **app 1**
1(g) **§2.52**
1(i) **§8.18**
1(j) **§§2.52, 8.46**
56(f) **§12.14**
57(a) **§9.20**
57(a)(6) **§14.16**
63(c)(5) **§8.18**
67 **§§7.6, 15.15, 15.36**
67(e) **§15.15**
72(b)(2) **§11.8**
72(b)(3) **§11.8**
72(e)(2)(B)(i) **§11.11**
72(e)(4)(A) **§11.11**
72(e)(4)(C) **§11.19**
72(e)(4)(C)(ii) **§11.19**
72(e)(4)(C)(iii) **§11.19**
72(q) **§11.11**
72(q)(2) **§11.11**
72(s) **§11.8**
79(b) **§10.56**
79(d) **§10.56**
79(e) **§10.56**
89 **§10.56**
89(b) **§10.56**
89(d) **§10.56**
89(e) **§10.56**
89(f) **§10.56**
89(h) **§10.56**
89(j)(1) **§10.56**

89(k) **§10.56**
101(a) **§§10.59, 12.14**
101(b)(3)(B) **§13.22**
101(f) **§10.59**
101(f)(1) **§10.59**
101(f)(3)(C) **§10.59**
101(f)(3)(G) **§10.59**
121 **§4.24**
151(d)(2) **§8.18**
163 **§§9.19A, 10.29**
163(h) **§§10.29, 15.15**
163(h)(2)(E) **§12.52**
164(a)(5) **§5.42**
168(e)(4)(H) **§15.27**
170 **§14.8**
170(b)(1)(C) **§14.12**
170(b)(1)(C)(ii) **§14.15**
170(b)(1)(C)(iii) **§14.13**
170(b)(1)(D)(ii) **§14.15**
170(e)(1)(B)(i) **§14.14**
170(e)(B)(1)(iii) **§14.11**
170(e)(5) **§14.11**
213(a) **§15.10**
213(c)(1) **§15.10**
213(c)(2) **§15.10**
219(c) **§13.20**
267(c)(4) **§14.11**
301 **§12.33**
302 **§12.33**
302(b)(1) **§12.33**

Treasury Regulations

§1.72-1(d) §11.8
§1.72-9 §§5.22, 11.15, 11.16
§1.79-0 §10.56
§1.79-1(b) §10.56
§1.79-1(c)(2) §10.56
§1.79-1(c)(3) §10.56
§1.79-3(d)(2) §10.56
§1.305(b)(2) §12.42
§1.642(g)-1(a)(2) §15.16
§1.661(a)-2(f)(3) §4.19
§1.664-4 §14.25
§1.706-1(c)(3)(iv) §12.24
§1.1001-2(b)(3) §14.17
§1.1001-2(B)(4)(iii) §8.23
§20.2031-7(f) app 2
§20.2039-4(a) §13.21
§20.2039-4(c) §13.21
§20.2039-4(e) §13.21
§20.2039-4(f) §13.21

§20.2056(b)-5(b) §4.22
§22.2056-1(b) §§4.22, 15.26
§25.2512-5 §8.50, app 2
§25.2512-9(f) §9.10
§25.2514-1(b)(2) §5.8
§25.2518-2(c)(4)(i) §15.38
§25.2518-2(c)(5) Ex. (9) §15.38
§25.2518-2(e)(2) Ex. (5) §15.38
§25.2518-3 §15.38
§25.2518-3(a)(2) §15.38
§25.2518-3(a)(iii) §15.49
§25.2518-3(c) §15.38
§25.2523(a)-1(d) §9.22

Proposed

§20.2056(b)-7(b) §§4.22, 15.26
§20.2056(b)-7(e) §4.24
§25.2523(f)-1(c)(2) §11.9

Revenue Rulings and Procedures

Rulings

55-117, 1955-1 CB 233 §4.31
67-74, 1967-1 CB 194 §4.19
76-490, 1976-2 CB 300 §10.56
77-85, 1977-1 CB 12 §11.11
79-353, 1979-2 CB 325 §5.14
79-376, 1979-2 CB 133 §12.38
80-274, 1980-2 CB 27 §11.11
81-31, 1981-1 CB 475 §12.48
81-225, 1981-2 CB 12 §11.11
82-55, 82-1 CB 12 §11.11
82-145, IRB 1982-31, 7 §10.57
82-182, IRB 1982-44 §12.52
83-108, IRB 1983-30, 14 §8.35
83-119, IRB 1983-3, 6 §12.42
83-120, IRB 1983-33, 8 §12.41
84-43, 1984-1 CB 27 §4.24
84-75, 1984-1 CB 193 §15.15
84-130, IRB 1984-35, 5 §10.56
84-147, 1984-2 CB 201 §10.56
84-179, 1984-2 CB 195
　§§10.41, 10.42
85-75, IRB 1985-23, 19 §15.27
85-88, IRB 1985-26 §8.35
85-169, IRB 1985-44 §12.52
86-82, 1986-1 CB 253 §8.41

87-75, IRB 1987-4 §2.24

Procedures

81-37, 1981-2 CB 592 §10.48
82-28, 1982-1 CB 480 §12.41
83-22, 1983-1 CB 680 §10.47

Letter Rulings

7806001 §8.48
7929054 §4.31
7947008 §10.47
8012129 §13.21
8021058 §10.56
8029054 §4.31
8119040 §4.31
8136022 §12.54
8145012 §8.48
8203009 §12.53
8223014 §11.13
8240055 §12.54
8301050 §§4.22, 15.26
8342008 §10.56
8447005 §2.3
8504011 §12.44
8509092 §15.38
8609005 §7.21A
8611006 §4.26
8701003 §12.47

Cases

A

Alexander, CS Estate of v Commr 82 TC 34 (1984) **§4.15**

B

Bailly, Estate of v Commr 81 TC 246 No 18 (1983) **§15.15**

Bloch, Jr, Harry, Estate of v Commr 78 TC 850 (1982) **§10.41**

Bright, Estate of v US 658 F2d 999 (5th Cir 1981) **§12.6**

Brown v Commr 241 F2d 827 (8th Cir 1957) **§9.19**

C

Christofferson v US 84-2 USTC ¶9990 (1984) **§11.11**

Clay, Estate of 86 TC 1266 (1986) **§10.14**

Commr v Tufts 456 US 960, 103 SCt 1826 (1983) **§14.17**

D

Dickman v Commr 465 US 330 (1984) (84-1 USTC ¶13,560) **§9.21**

Dickman v Commr 82-2 USTC ¶13,501 (11th Cir 1982) **§9.21**

Diedrich v Commr 457 US 191 (1982) **§8.1**

DiMarco, Estate of 87 TC 653 (1986) **§12.48**

E

Epp v Commr 78 TC 801 (1982) **§7.6**

F

Fabric, Estate of 83 TC 932 (1984) **§11.13**

First National Bank of Denver v US 648 F2d 1286 (10th Cir 1981) **§5.14**

Frederick C Braun, Jr 48 TCM 210 (1984) **§9.13**

Index

Entries in this supplement index reflect new areas of material in the supplement that are not referenced by the main index in the bound volume. Please refer both to the main index and this supplement index to insure complete research.